T0339536

Cambridge Elements ≡

Elements in Women in Music
edited by
Rhiannon Mathias
Bangor University, UK

GRAŻYNA BACEWICZ, THE 'FIRST LADY OF POLISH MUSIC'

Diana Ambache
www.womenofnote.co.uk/

CAMBRIDGE
UNIVERSITY PRESS

CAMBRIDGE
UNIVERSITY PRESS

University Printing House, Cambridge CB2 8BS, United Kingdom

One Liberty Plaza, 20th Floor, New York, NY 10006, USA

477 Williamstown Road, Port Melbourne, VIC 3207, Australia

314–321, 3rd Floor, Plot 3, Splendor Forum, Jasola District Centre, New Delhi – 110025, India

103 Penang Road, #05–06/07, Visioncrest Commercial, Singapore 238467

Cambridge University Press is part of the University of Cambridge.

It furthers the University's mission by disseminating knowledge in the pursuit of education, learning, and research at the highest international levels of excellence.

www.cambridge.org
Information on this title: www.cambridge.org/9781108823111
DOI: 10.1017/9781108913485

First published 2022

A catalogue record for this publication is available from the British Library.

ISBN 978-1-108-82311-1 Paperback
ISSN 2633-6871 (online)
ISSN 2633-6863 (print)

Grażyna Bacewicz, The 'First Lady of Polish Music'

Elements in Women in Music

DOI: 10.1017/9781108913485
First published online: July 2022

Diana Ambache
www.womenofnote.co.uk/
Author for correspondence: Diana Ambache, diana@ambache.co.uk

Abstract: This Element explores the life and work of Grażyna Bacewicz (1909–1969) as a composer, violinist, pianist, and author. She lived a remarkable life in Poland, navigating the complex world of Polish communist society and Soviet dominance after World War II, and she brought Polish music to wider European attention. The Element also describes the historical context of her life, her major achievements, and the language and development of her compositions, which attracted notable interest in Polish musical life. She wrote a wide range of pieces, making a significant contribution to the string repertoire, with important string quartets and violin works. In her sixty years she achieved impressive triumphs as a woman composer, served the Polish Composers Union, and often judged major international competitions.

This Element also has a video abstract: www.cambridge.org/ambache_abstract

Keywords: Bacewicz, Poland, composer, violin, strings

ISBNs: 9781108823111 (PB), 9781108913485 (OC)
ISSNs: 2633-6871 (online), 2633-6863 (print)

Contents

Figure 1 Grażyna Bacewicz by B J Doris, 1959.

Introduction

Grażyna Bacewicz (1909–69) was the foremost Polish woman composer of the twentieth century. Although some sixty CDs of her music are listed on Amazon, it is still not part of the established canon. As a virtuoso violinist, she wrote beautifully for string instruments, so it is puzzling that string players are not familiar with her work. This volume seeks to dispel some of these issues.

Opinions about Bacewicz's music come from various sources – woodworm, the critics, performers, prize-givers – and here are some of those opinions. She had just given an inspired performance as the soloist in Karol Szymanowski's *Violin Concerto No. 1*, when, on returning to the artist's room, she found a small, unimposing man, who introduced himself as the Custodian of the Museum of String Instruments. He said that quite often he played one of her violin compositions, and he explained why: 'I discovered some woodworm in one of the old instruments so I take all the violins in turn and play your piece. The woodworm do not like your music and run away in panic. I came to thank you.'[1]

The 'woodworm' were out of step with the musical world, who appreciated both Bacewicz's creativity and her warm personality. She won numerous Polish awards (several from the communist government) and half a dozen accolades of European origin. Prizes from the national administration suggest political approval, while awards from Western Europe were a dispassionate appreciation of her skills without any ideological background. Her *Violin Concerto No. 7* (1965) won her the biggest prize – the Gold Medal at the Queen Elizabeth International Competition in Brussels. Her position as a leader in Polish national culture came from her many talents (which we have just listed); she was the doyenne of Polish music of the twentieth century. Her story is remarkable, and more performances of her music are needed to bring attention to its extraordinary integrity and personal expression.

Bacewicz's remarkable life included impressive achievements, and her music is appealing in its vitality, naturalness, and directness. In 2016, the Ambache Ensemble recorded a CD of some of her chamber works, and comments in the reviews included phrases such as 'the genius of Polish composer Bacewicz' and 'a perfect introduction to an important twentieth-century composer'.[2] There was little knowledge of her work at that time, and there is still not a lot now. Given that her music is accessible and attractive, it is unclear why this is so. One reason must be that, even in the twenty-first century, women are still not taken as

---

[1] Cited in 'Woodworm Don't Like Your Music', BBC Radio 3 'Composer of the Week – Bacewicz', programme 5 (29 May 2015): www.bbc.co.uk/programmes/b05wxt9f/episodes/guide.

[2] Reviews from *BBC Music Magazine* (March 2017) and *The Arts Desk* (March 2017).

Figure 2 Photo of Bacewicz by Andrzej Ziborski

seriously as men. Then, there is the problem of the musical canon – a kind of catch-22: if you are in, you are in; if you are not, it is difficult to get in. Possibly, performers and audiences still have a tendency to be oriented to the old favourites in German and Italian music. At any rate, there are many male and female composers who are not given due recognition, and they also need contemporary champions.

Some recognition has come for Bacewicz, of course. In 2019 (110 years after her birth and 50 years after her death), there were special Bacewicz celebrations in Poland. The Polish pianist Krystian Zimerman has toured Poland, other European countries, and America performing her music, and has recorded sonatas and quintets for Deutsche Grammophon, receiving fine notices; however, Zimerman's biography on Deutsche Grammophon's website does not mention Bacewicz. Interest lapsed, and she was neglected once again. It is hard to understand the reasons why, because Bacewicz can be recommended for so many things. Exceptionally talented both as a violinist and as a composer, her music is pleasing and straightforward; she developed her own musical language, absorbing contemporary ideas while maintaining her authentic voice. Her natural interest in Polish folk music was one aspect that helped her navigate the difficult and restricted times in Communist Poland, particularly under Stalinist rule. The prizes she won for her compositions illustrate that she was valued, and a Polish postal stamp of 2009 recognised the 100th anniversary of her birth. Even so, this author thinks she has not received the attention she deserves.

This Element is laid out chronologically, starting with Bacewicz's birth in Łódź, studies in Warsaw, and life during World War II in Section 1. In the decade following the war, she guided her composing career through the restrictive world of Polish socialist realism and communist control (Section 2). Her last fifteen years are considered in two connected parts in Section 3 (Parts 1 and 2), covering her experiments with sonorism and serialism, and the founding of the Warsaw Autumn Festival (with Tadeusz Baird and Kazimierz Serocki). To conclude, there is a description of her legacy in both Poland and the wider world. The compositions are described within the context of her European setting, and her personal circumstances are given as a background to her achievements.

Social attitudes have limited women's activities. The musical arena is crowded, and twists of fate have made life difficult for female composers. However, people are now increasingly recognising a wider field of contributors, and some of the main UK organisations (such as the BBC) are gradually increasing their inclusion of their music. Radio 3's 'Composer of the Week' featured Bacewicz in May 2015, and each day's broadcast had an expressive title: 'An Unseen Little Engine'; 'A Mood of Determined Resistance'; 'A False Dawn'; 'Opening the Modernist Floodgates'; and 'Woodworms Don't Like Your Music'.[3] Curiously though, the BBC Proms, 'the World's Greatest Classical Music Festival', has given only one performance of her music: the *Piano Quintet No. 1* in 2019, at the Cadogan Hall.[4]

I mentioned earlier that her string works are not generally known to performers. Any string player would be pleased to study and play Bacewicz's works, as they are so gratefully written. The accessibility of her style means that her pieces are not 'difficult' modern music, and her use of folk ideas makes them immediately resonant. Her excellent compositions would appear more frequently in concerts if more players, teachers, and programmers were familiar with them. Her substantial contribution to the string repertoire alone includes seven string quartets, five violin sonatas, a *Quartet for Four Violins*, and a *Quartet for Four Cellos*; this music is very rewarding for both players and audiences.

Considered her finest work, Bacewicz's *Concerto for String Orchestra* (1948) has several YouTube performances. At the time of this writing (during the coronavirus pandemic) there are no live performances, but the last one

---

[3] A Radio 3 'Composer of the Week' highlights programme, featuring sections from all five programmes, is available for download: www.bbc.co.uk/programmes/p02sln1f.

[4] See the BBC Proms Performance Archive: www.bbc.co.uk/programmes/articles/3SsklRvCSPvfHr13wgz6HCJ/proms-performance-archive.

livestreamed online was in October 2020.[5] Her *Concerto for String Orchestra*, and her music in general, communicates a rare combination of energy and honesty; the slow movements come from the heart. Her natural affinity with the traditional music of her country imbued her own music with local colour in rhythm and melody. Studying with Nadia Boulanger in Paris brought her in touch with the neoclassical style, which suited her musical temperament. As musical language changed, serialism and sonorism were explored; she took what interested her and absorbed it into her own manner. This combination of the national element, current ideas, and her own voice added up to quirky, witty, exciting, and original music of a personal nature. She explained her vitality as coming from what she called a 'motorek':

> I possess a little unseen engine, and thanks to it I accomplish a task in ten minutes that it takes others an hour or more; I normally do not walk but I run; I speak fast; even my pulse beats faster than others and I was born in the seventh month. I was born for action, not for empty talk ... There is only one essential needed: 'motorek ... ' – without it don't bother.[6]

Her death just before becoming sixty was a surprise, and many people were shocked by losing her. Here is an account from her colleague, Polish composer and conductor Jan Krenz (1926–2020):

> The effects of her life are simply extraordinary. She was, of course, very industrious, but also very well organised. She knew how to use time ... If she got involved in something, she did it authentically, with full devotion. Sometimes famous artists just give their name, while others do the work for them. But it was not Grażyna's case. She was able to happily combine many activities, achieving good results. She had a smile and cheerfulness for everyone. She never revealed any of her dilemmas, personal problems, which bother us, artists, and which certainly weren't spared her ... She was emancipated through and through, her natural traits included personal independence and self-reliance.[7]

Before presenting her story, here is a brief overview of Polish music.[8] Starting at the end of the nineteenth century, music was based in the conservatories, music

---

[5] Livestream concert given by The Orchestra Now, conducted by Zachary Schwartzman (17 October 2020): www.youtube.com/watch?v=TBwf-ldcd1g.

[6] Grażyna Bacewicz, *A Distinguishing Mark (Znak szczególny)*, 3rd ed., trans. A. Clarke and A. Cienski (Orleans, Canada: Krzys Chmiel, 2004), pp. 25–6.

[7] Jan Krenz in conversation with Elżbieta Markowska in *Rozmowy o muzyce polskiej*, (Kraków: PWM, 1996), pp. 65 and 67. See also 'Bacewicz: Personality-Human Being', *Polmic.pl*: https://bacewicz.polmic.pl/en/human-being.

[8] Detailed accounts about Polish music can be found in the following volumes: Maja Trochimczyk (ed.), *After Chopin: Essays in Polish Music*, vol. 6 (Los Angeles: Polish Music Center at USC, 2000) and Adrian Thomas, *Polish Music Since Szymanowski* (Cambridge: Cambridge University Press, 2005).

societies, and the development of choirs and musical literacy. Gathering together to rejuvenate their music, the 'Young Poland' group (*Młoda Polska*) followed new directions.[9] Mieczysław Karlowicz (1876–1909) and Ludomir Różcki (1883–1953) wrote symphonic poems. Ignacy Paderewski (1860–1941) was a composer, international virtuoso pianist, and an important Polish statesman; his opera, *Manru,* was performed at the Metropolitan Opera in New York in 1902. Karol Szymanowski (1882–1937) composed operas, symphonies, violin concertos, a ballet (*Harnasie*), and a *Stabat Mater.* Perceived as the most famous 'modern' Polish composer of his day, Szymanowski's late romantic style developed to include impressionist and oriental ideas, and he was influenced by folk music of the Górale people (of southern Poland). Originating from the plains of Mazovia around Warsaw, the 'mazur' (mazurka) had become Poland's most typical musical/cultural export, largely thanks to internationally celebrated Fryderyk Chopin (1810–49). Also originating from Mazovia was the 'oberek' folk dance, and the fast and syncopated 'krakowiak' came from Krakow, further in the north. Many pieces by Chopin, Szymanowski, and Bacewicz incorporate characteristics of these and other Polish folk tunes.

Figure 3 Karol Szymanowski

[9] See Teresa Chylińska, 'Young Poland', *Grove Music Online*: https://doi.org/10.1093/gmo/9781561592630.article.49416

To provide a foretaste of the historical and political background that will be encountered in this Element, it should be noted that Poland first became independent from the Russian-controlled *Mitteleuropa* in 1918 – when Bacewicz was nine years old. Following Independence, the Polish population centres (notably Warsaw, Kraków, and Łódź) grew, and the economy improved until the Great Depression that darkened Europe (1929–39). Increasingly aggressive, Nazi Germany invaded Poland in 1939, and Warsaw fell on 27 September. Many cultural institutions were closed at this time, and the careers of many musicians came to an end. In the underground resistance movement there was a clandestine Music Council, and Bacewicz hosted some of their off-the-record concerts, keeping Polish music alive. The Warsaw Uprising of 1944 ended with the Germans destroying the city. A communist government was agreed upon at the end of World War II, and there was a particularly oppressive period under Stalin's control (1948–53) with the diktats of socialist realism, when the creative process was compromised by state censorship. However, there was a liberalising trend from 1956 onward. Started in 1956, the Warsaw Autumn was a major international festival of contemporary music, and Bacewicz was part of its creation.

Times have changed, and we can now appreciate the strength Bacewicz brought to the many challenges of her life. She was, and still is, an inspiration to musicians, Poles, and people in general in the way she led her life as a composer, violinist, humanitarian, and ambassador for her country. This Element aspires to contribute to her regaining recognition.

1 Early Maturity to 1945

Grażyna Bacewicz was born in 1909 in Łódź, Poland, when her country was still partitioned between Austria, Prussia, and Russia.[10] Both her parents were musical, and they gave her a well-grounded childhood. Her mother, Maria Modlińska (1871–1958), the daughter of a Warsaw engineer, had a cultured upbringing, worked in bank administration, and was a fine amateur pianist. In 1903, Maria married Vincas Bacevičius (1875–1952), a Lithuanian and music graduate of the Teacher Training College in Veiveriai (Kaunas, Lithuania).[11] Bacewicz was the third of their four children (two boys and two girls), and the children's names – Kiejstut, Vytautus, and

---

[10] Łódź is Poland's third most populated city, after Warsaw and Kraków. The name Łódź translates as 'boat', and the inhabitants call themselves *Łódzianie*, the 'boat people' – possibly referring to the historic multicultural nature of the city's inhabitants.

[11] From 1795, the Polish–Lithuanian Commonwealth was dissolved by Austria, Prussia, and Poland, effectively erasing them from the map. In 1885, Russian became the official language in Lithuania, and many Lithuanians emigrated. Vincas shared the fate of other teachers in Lithuania in being forbidden to teach, and was deported to Poland in 1899.

Grażyna – were more Lithuanian than Polish, except for the youngest, Wanda.[12] Bacewicz's eldest brother, Kiejstut, said of family life:

> We owe to both our parents our respect for work and order, for learning, art and human values in general. We inherited musical dispositions from both our father and our mother, but that genetic legacy is not all. What really affected the development of the children's personalities was the atmosphere of their home and educational effort on the part of both parents.[13]

Passionate about music, Vincas Bacevičius pushed all his children to practice and play from an early age. Bacewicz later recalled that she was engulfed in sound as a baby, and two of her short stories refer to her father's teaching and devotion to music. In 'A Lyrical Introduction', a grouchy relative was convinced he was harming the children by submerging them in music from a very young age.[14] 'Still More Lyrical' spoke of how her younger sister, aged four, was pushed to play in the family string quartet. Dreaming of poetry, Wanda hid under the table, hoping not to be found.[15]

Figure 4 Vincas Bacevičius, 1920s

---

[12] Grażyna is derived from the Lithuanian adjective *gražus* meaning pretty.

[13] Kiejstut Bacewicz, 'Wspomnienie o braci Vytautasie Baceviciusie', in Krzysztof Droba, ed., *W kregu muzyki litewskiej* (Krakow: Akademia muzyczna w Krakowie, 1997). Kiejstut Bacewicz (1904–93) went on to become a highly esteemed pianist, composer, and teacher in Polish musical life. His full biography can be found on the website of the Grażyna and Kiejstut Bacewicz Academy of Music, Łódź: www.amuz.lodz.pl/en/52-system-en-gb/academy.

[14] Bacewicz, 'A Lyrical Introduction' in *A Distinguishing Mark*, p. 7.

[15] Bacewicz, 'Still More Lyrical', ibid., p. 8.

Vincas taught Bacewicz the violin and the piano as a child, and she was immediately fond of the violin. All four children played chamber music (in the aforementioned family string quartet), both in their home and in public. Vincas wanted to prepare his children for the Conservatory and so urged them on: there was little free time. Bacewicz said, 'from the earliest days we lived in a world of sound because of his love of music'.[16] She probably learnt her work ethic from him.

Bacewicz showed considerable musical talent early on: a printed programme lists the seven-year-old appearing as a pianist and violinist during *Podwieczorek Muzyczny* (Tea Music) in June 1916. She commenced regular schooling in 1919, entering the Humanistic Secondary School in Łódź, and the Helena Kijeńska-Dobkiewiczowa Music Conservatory to study violin, piano, and theory. Regarded as something of a child prodigy, she played several violin concerti with the orchestra at the Kijeńska-Dobkiewiczowa Conservatory before the age of twelve. She then started to develop an interest in writing music and began composing from the age of thirteen.[17] She soon discovered pleasure in creating instrumental pieces, and her early works include *Four Preludes* for piano (1921) and *Preludium and Fugue* for piano (1927) – welcoming the challenge of writing fugues. *Five Pieces for Four Flutes* (1929) followed, and also a *Sinfonietta* for chamber orchestra (1929). However, she wasn't always pleased with her compositions and sometimes discounted them from her oeuvre. A couple of string quartets (1930 and 1931) went that way.

Independence

Poland's national symbol is the white-tailed eagle, denoting vitality, strength, and tenacity: these were all qualities Grażyna Bacewicz possessed in abundance. Her intense early music education coincided with momentous changes for Poland. In November 1918, when she was nine years old, Poland achieved national independence (with the Treaty of Versailles) after 123 years of occupation by Prussians, Russians, and Austrians. This was a significant moment for all Polish people, and the liberation of their country had profound creative effects, including a sense of responsibility for Polish music. Uniquely, Ignacy Paderewski (1869–1941) was both a musician – a composer and an international touring virtuoso pianist – and an important Polish statesman: he was intimately involved with events leading up to Polish independence and served for a time as

---

[16] Ibid.

[17] Bacewicz spoke about this in a radio interview in 1964, reprinted in *Ruch Muzyczny* 1989, no. 3, p. 7.

Figure 5 The Polish Eagle

Poland's first prime minister.[18] Even as a child, Bacewicz would probably have been aware of Paderewski's celebrated performances of the music of Chopin, a composer whose influence on generations of Polish composers (including Bacewicz's) was both lasting and profound. One of the first Polish composers to use elements of Polish folk music in his works, Chopin also was a national symbol of resistance and a source of cultural identity.

Regarding influential female role models, the young Bacewicz would likely have known of two-time Nobel Prize-winner Marie Curie (1867–1934) and of Polish composer and virtuoso pianist Maria Szymanowska (1789–1831), who was described by Goethe as 'a great talent bordering on madness'.[19] Maria Konopnicka (1842–1910), a poet, author, and activist for Polish independence, was also familiar to Bacewicz: she later wrote the music for a 1960 film based on Konopnicka's story *Marysia i krasnoludki* (*Maria and the Dwarfs*). Other possible role models on Bacewicz's radar may have been the composer Tekla Bądarzewska-Baranowska (1829/1832–61), whose most famous piece, *The Maiden's Prayer*, first published in Warsaw in 1856, was still selling well in

---

[18] For further information, see Jim Samson, 'Paderewsk, Ignacy Jan', *Grove Music Online*: https://doi.org/10.1093/gmo/9781561592630.article.20672; and 'Jan Ignacy Paderewski', Polish Music Center: https://polishmusic.usc.edu/research/composers/ignacy-jan-paderewski.

[19] 'das größte Talent gleichsam nur als Folie', letter from Goethe to his daughter-in-law Ottilie (18 August 1823), cited in E. Zapolska Chapelle, trans. F. Goodman, 'Maria Szymanowska (1789–1831): A Woman of Europe': www.maria-szymanowska.eu/kto-to-jest-en?cmn_id=1017&ph_content_start=show.

Figure 6 Marie Curie

Melbourne, Australia, in 1924; and Regine Wieniawska (1879–1932), daughter of Polish composer Henryk Wieniawski, who composed songs, violin pieces, and orchestral works under the pseudonym of Poldowski.

A Family Break-up and Warsaw

The years 1918–20 also saw Lithuania gain independence, something which prompted Bacewicz's father to give thought to returning to his home nation. Vincas eventually left Poland for Lithuania in 1923 – when Bacewicz was fourteen – and settled in Kaunas, where he worked for the Lithuanian education system for the next twenty-nine years, until his death. Although the intention probably was that his family would join him in Lithuania, this was not to be. Vytautas (the second eldest son) chose to follow his father back to Lithuania in 1926. While there, as well as giving piano recitals, he helped develop original radical composition ideas in his new country.[20] Bacewicz, her mother, and her two other siblings remained in Poland, eventually moving from Łódź to

---

[20] Bacewicz's second eldest brother, Vytautas Bacevičius (1905–70), became a Lithuanian composer and pianist, who established his career in Lithuania before permanently settling in America after the outbreak of World War II. For further information, see 'Vytautas Bacevičius', *Music Information Centre Lithuania*: www.mic.lt/en/database/classical/composers/bacevicius.

Warsaw. Her eldest brother, Kiejstut, later commented on his family's geographic split:

> It is all too clear that, in our civilised world, each individual himself or herself decides on his or her national allegiance, on their ties with a particular historical and cultural tradition. It is all a matter of subjectivity, of the sense of an inner connection and affinity to a particular ethnic community and the values it represents. The sovereign right of self-determination is at the same time the right of a free choice of one's development, self-realisation and co-responsibility for the chosen community. The fact that members of a single family represent different nationalities is far from unique.[21]

Although family members visited each other, spending their summers in Lithuania, the break-up was probably challenging for the teenage Bacewicz. Later, she regularly gave concerts in Lithuania and included aspects of Lithuanian culture in several of her youthful compositions. Her *Variations on a Lithuanian Folksong* (1934) for violin and piano illustrates the connection with her father's origins. It is an engaging set of variations. Concise, like a series of compact miniatures, and following the original theme, the variations create a broad range of moods, including a Pierrot-like Menuetto and a slightly ethereal Berceuse. When recording them for our Bacewicz CD, David Juritz and I were impressed with how quickly she conjured up the atmosphere of each variation.[22]

Having chosen to remain in Poland, Kiejstut studied at the Conservatory of Music in Warsaw from 1924, and Bacewicz entered the Conservatory a little later, in 1928.[23] It was at the Conservatory that Bacewicz first met Karol Szymanowski, Poland's most celebrated composer at this time. Szymanowski served as the Conservatory's Rector from 1930 to 1932, and his music then became an important source of influence on Bacewicz. Her assigned composition tutor, Kazimierz Sikorski (1895–1986), also was a strong guide during these years, giving her an understanding of the importance of musical form, and concurrently she studied violin with Józef Jarzębski (1878–1955) and piano with Józef Turczyński (1884–1953). Widening her horizons, Bacewicz joined a philosophy course at Warsaw University but gave it up over a year later due to

---

[21] Kiejstut Bacewicz, cited in Malgorzata Janicka-Slysz, 'The Letters of Grażyna Bacewicz and Vytautas Bacevičius', Internationale Arbeitsgemeinschaft für die Musikgeschichte in Mittel- und Osteuropa an der Universität Leipzig (2017): https://core.ac.uk/download/pdf/226124382.pdf.

[22] Diana Ambache, 'Grażyna Bacewicz: Chamber Music' CD (2017): www.womenofnote.co.uk.

[23] She stayed with Kiejstut and his wife (in a rented flat at Bobra Street 2) from July in that year, before moving to a flat in Długa Street with her mother and Wanda, who had relocated from Łódź.

other requirements. Indeed, she also stopped playing the piano, eventually graduating from the Warsaw Conservatory in 1932 with top marks for diplomas in violin and composition.

The Fryderyk Chopin University of Music (formerly, the Warsaw Conservatory) holds a page on Bacewicz's life, written by herself, dated '18. IX.1930' and catalogued in their archives.[24] It lists studying at the Humanistic Junior High School; Professor Helena Kijeńska-Dobkiewiczowa teaching her at the Łódź Conservatory; her 1928 Secondary School Certificate; passing her exam in Sikorski's class in the Warsaw Conservatory; joining Jarzębski's violin class there in 1929; and going to visit her father in Lithuania in March 1930. It should be noted that prior to entering the Warsaw Conservatory, Bacewicz had already established a profile as a talented violinist: from 1925 to 1927 she played with the Łódź Philharmonic Orchestra, and often, with her brother Kiejstut as pianist, she performed in Poland, Lithuania, and Latvia.[25] In 1932, however, Bacewicz gave her composition diploma recital at the Conservatory, and the programme included her cantata *De profundis de clamavi ad Te Domine* for solo voices, choir, and orchestra (1932), *Sinfonietta* (1932), *String Quartet* (1931), and *Sonata for Violin and Piano* (1932).[26] The concert was the start of things to come.

Further Studies in Paris, Compositions, and First Prizes

Szymanowski advised young musicians to go abroad to widen their experience, and he particularly recommended the teacher Nadia Boulanger. Previously, Germany had been favoured as an educational destination; but as the looser, romantic expression of the nineteenth century developed, Germany became less popular in Poland. This sense of Germany's having lost the clarity of the eighteenth century led to its rejection as an educational destination. By contrast, the path of concise logic produced the neoclassical movement, which was developed in France. Even after the *Années folles* of the 1920s, Paris was the cultural hub of Europe and still a mecca for artists. So, Paris it was for Bacewicz. The balanced forms and clear thematic processes of neoclassicism seemed to suit her musical temperament and free her from romanticism.

Boulanger's clarity, insight, and drive helped to shape the work of two generations of Polish composers; her Polish students had included Kazimierz Sikorski (Bacewicz's composition tutor) and Zygmund Mycielski, who later became editor--in-chief of the music journal *Ruch Muzyczny*. At the École Normale de Musique

---

[24] Archive of the Warsaw National Conservatory of Music, Students File no. 96/46.

[25] After graduating from Warsaw Conservatory, Kiejstut worked as a music teacher in Kaunas, Lithuania, before returning to Poland in 1935.

[26] Archive of the Warsaw National Conservatory of Music, Concert Programme.

in Paris, Bacewicz studied composition with Boulanger and violin with André Touret from 1932 to 1933. Boulanger was an exacting teacher who knew how to direct her students, with clear guidance on melody, harmony, rhythm, and orchestration. She would have encouraged Bacewicz to develop a musical language that was uniquely her own. Boulanger's enthusiasm and strength of conviction was a fine role model of musicianship. She seems to have been particularly fond of her Polish students and said that Bacewicz came with sound foundations: 'When as a young girl she came to Paris, she showed great talent, which was to develop constantly for many years. As most of my Polish students, Grażyna had received a solid education, both classical and contemporary.'[27]

During her time in Paris, Bacewicz composed her *Wind Quintet* (1932), the *Sonatina for Piano*, and the *Children's Suite* (*Suita Dziecięca*) – both of the latter works in 1933.[28] The *Sonatina* shows some French influence, has a doleful Lento slow movement, and returns to Bacewicz's Polish origins with a sparky, oberek finale.[29] Bacewicz showed an interest in her national folk music long before the interwar government requirement to include it. She probably warmed to the oberek because of its lively energy, matching her own vitality; she spoke of doing everything fast, and this corresponded with the high-spirited folk manner of this dance.

The *Children's Suite* is a collection of short character pieces for piano, with titles indicating the wide range of ideas: 'Prelude', 'March', 'Waltz', 'Berceuse', 'Burlesque', 'Minuet', 'Gavotte', and 'Scherzino'. Their rhythmic energy and vitality, simple lyrical melodies, well-controlled tonality, and careful treatment of dissonance might be linked to Boulanger's influence. The 'Waltz' is a rocking lullaby; the 'Burlesque' is light and whimsical, with syncopations; the 'Gavotte' illustrates her tendency toward parody by making a skittish allusion to the 'Gavotte' in Prokofiev's *'Classical' Symphony* of 1916–17.

Her *Wind Quintet* was the first of her compositions to win a prize – First Prize (1,000 francs) in the 1933 Paris competition, Concours de la Société 'Aide aux femmes de professions libres': this gave her a new sense of

---

[27] Boulanger quoted in *Dla ludzi zawsze mam twarz pogodną . . . Grażyna Bacewicz* (documentary film), directed by D. Pawelec, scenario by M. Gąsiorowska and D. Pawelec, Telewizja Polska – Program II, 1999: www.youtube.com/watch?v=0HAGaACyt94.

[28] Bacewicz's symphonic poem *Convoi de Joie* was also composed in 1933 but is not listed by her publisher, PWM. According to her biographer, Małgorzata Gąsiorowska, she didn't attach much importance to it, although it was played twice in 1936, in Latvia and Poland. See Gąsiorowska, *Bacewicz* (Krakow: PWM, 1999), p. 84.

[29] The 'oberek' is the fastest of mazurka-rhythm-based dances from Poland – a lively national dance in three-time, with features including lightness and agility, and repetitions of melodic and rhythmic figures. See M. Trochimczyk, 'Oberek (Obertas)', Polish Music Center: https://polish music.usc.edu/research/dances/oberek.

independence and freedom. The piece showed impressive assurance for such a youthful composer (aged twenty-four), with well-characterised woodwind writing, unusual for a non-wind player. It is composed in a neoclassical manner with clarity, wit, and brevity. In both thematic and tonal outlines, the Allegro sticks to the sonata principle, with a *moto perpetuo* quality in the quavers. The Andante – Air has a solemn horn statement, followed by a folk-inspired bassoon solo. The tiny Allegretto is more playful. The opening theme of the spirited Vivo has a quasi-fugal presentation, then attractively catchy rhythms and airy melodies.

It is worth stressing at this point that, although Bacewicz's music at this time embodies the mainstream neoclassical outlook of 1920s European musical thought, the neoclassical tag has been rather overused in describing her music. The style simply suited her affection for balanced form, and it is notable that the composer herself objected to the label when it was carelessly applied:

> For ten years I have been watching a certain phenomenon in our musical environment that concerns me (I apologize for writing about myself) and I have to confess, that with every year that passes by, a bigger astonishment overwhelms me. In ancient post-war times my output was labelled as neo-classical. In those times it was not baseless. But my work has undergone changes . . . A label once given is still current for them [the researchers]. This way the actual state of affairs is distorted. For nine years I have found this fact amusing. Now it has stopped amusing me.[30]

Her interest in structure, motivic techniques, rhythmic energy, and fondness for contrapuntal textures overlapped with that of Bohuslav Martinů (1890–1959) and Paul Hindemith (1895–1963). Mid-period Bartók was another influence, which showed in her use of bracing and dynamic dissonances, and (naturally) the assimilation of folk music. Bartók has been called the greatest composer of string quartets in the twentieth century; Bacewicz may be the second. As Poland came under the influence of the Soviet Union, it is likely that Bacewicz would also have known Shostakovich's quartets, beginning with No. 1 in 1938.

The Violin

Violin concerts continued to be an important part of Bacewicz's life. After leaving Paris in 1933, she made a recital tour of southern France, Spain,

---

[30] Bacewicz, letter to the editors of *Informator Muzyki Polskiej*, as cited in K. Bartos, 'The National Element in Grazyna Bacewicz's Music', *Meakultura* (29 September 2013): http://meakultura.pl /artykul/the-national-element-in-grazyna-bacewiczs-music-711.

Mallorca, and Italy with the pianist Jerzy Sulikowski (b. 1938), a member of the Association of Young Polish Musicians in Paris. Returning to Łódź, she was offered a position at the Helena Kijeńska-Dobkiewiczowa Conservatory to teach violin, harmony, and counterpoint. During the academic year 1934–5, she taught a violin class there but then left the Conservatory to devote herself to composing and violin playing.

Her experience of being an outstanding player undoubtedly led her to create a substantial and expressive oeuvre for violin. With pianist Jerzy Lefeld, she gave a recital on 10 May 1934 at the Warsaw Conservatory, consisting of all her major works for violin and piano.[31] The concert was announced in the *Kurier Poznański* and was widely acclaimed by critics.[32] The reviewer in the *Warsaw Courier* stated:

> This composer has no need for sensational effects and is to be commended on the beauty and seriousness of the work. There is a sense of youth in the composition while simultaneously there is a high degree of maturity. The musical impressions will overwhelm you and the musical thoughts will absorb you. She has a lot to say and she already knows how to say it well.[33]

The May concert included her two capriccios for violin and piano (1932 and 1934), her *Sonatina for Piano,* the *Children's Suite, Scherzo* for piano (1934), as well as her *Wind Quintet* and other pieces. The concert was recalled by Witold Lutosławski (1913–94), then a student at Conservatory:

> I remember that evening really vividly due to the fact that, as a then-student of Jerzy Lefeld, I turned pages of the score when he was accompanying Grażyna. She played, among other works, her violin Capriccios – compositions going far beyond a traditional concept of that virtuoso form. What particularly delighted me was a miniature of peculiar beauty entitled *Witraż,* woven out of colourful and delicate, wing-like sonorities.[34]

Written about the time of her graduation in 1932, *Witraż (Stained Glass)* is, naturally, about glass and, for her, was a rare departure from the tradition of naming instrumental pieces using strictly musical terms. Some possible Szymanowski influence may be detectable here. In this period, she often played his 'The Fountain of Arethusa' (from *Mythes*, Op. 30, 1915), and she was

---

[31] Jerzy Lefeld (1898–1980) was a Polish composer, pianist, and music teacher; he both studied and taught at the Warsaw Conservatory.

[32] The original *Kurier Poznański* announcement is reproduced in 'Bacewicz – First Successes', *Polmic.pl*: https://bacewicz.polmic.pl/en/first-successes.

[33] F. Szopski, as cited in Judith Rosen, *Grażyna Bacewicz: Her Life and Works* (Los Angeles: Polish Music Center at USC, 1984). https://polishmusic.usc.edu/research/publications/polish-music-journal/vol5no1/grazyna-bacewicz-life-and-works.

[34] Lutosławski, *Ruch Muzyczny* (15 April 1969), cited in 'Bacewicz – First Successes', *Polmic.pl.*

admired for the way she brought out its colouristic qualities. Szymanowski said that *Witraż* was 'a completely exceptional composition – ethereal (only 30 bars long), swaying, full of Art Nouveau ornaments and colours – it seems to be a nostalgic memory of the times not so distant, the times of her fascination with impressionistic-exotic'.[35]

Paris and the Wieniawski International Violin Competition

In 1934, Bacewicz returned to Paris to study with the great Hungarian violin teacher Carl Flesch (1873–1944).[36] He was a stern and exacting mentor, regularly interrupting the playing; and yet he inspired her to compose a *Partita* for violin and piano (1934, unpublished). Bacewicz premièred this work in 1935 – again, partnered by Lefeld – at a Warsaw concert organised by the Polish Music Publishers. The review of this concert in the *Kurier Warszawski* stated that:

> The talent of Grażyna Bacewicz leads her onto paths of sincerity, removes all artificiality, all pursuit of dramatic effects, which must be acknowledged and encouraged. A hint of beauty and seriousness marks her talent. *Partita* makes such a grand impression because two things are apparent in it; exact, logical form and exciting content. There is youthfulness in this piece, but there is also a high level of maturity; there is an overwhelming reflection and interesting leading ideas.[37]

Bacewicz's next composition, *Three Songs* ('The Mirage'; 'Another'; 'Solitude'), was based on a tenth-century Arabic text. Originally for tenor and piano, in 1938 it was rewritten for voice and orchestra. She was particularly interested in Arabic and Hindu cultures. Earlier, Bacewicz's admiration for the poetry of Rabindranath Tagore (1861–1941) had led her to set a song on his 1915 poem 'Speak to Me, My Love', composed in 1935, the year before her marriage to Andrzej Biernacki.

Her *Three Caricatures* for orchestra (1932, unpublished) were performed in Vilnius, Lithuania, in January 1934 under the baton of her brother Vytautas. He was principally a pianist and not a regular conductor, but did some conducting in Kaunas and, on this occasion, was furthering his sister's music.[38] There are also newspaper reports of her concerts in Kaunas in the

---

[35] Szymanowski, cited in Gąsiorowska, *Bacewicz*, p. 84.

[36] Carl Flesch was famous as both a player and a teacher. His texts, such as *Die Kunst des Violinspiels* (1923), are standard treatises on violin technique.

[37] Review (10 May 1934) in 'Bacewicz, 1929–1938', *Polmic.pl*: https://bacewicz.polmic.pl/1929-1938.

[38] V. Bacevičus, 'Wystepy Grazyny Bacewicz na Litwie' in Vytautas Bacevičus, f. 118, ap. 1, b. 188, l. 1, Lithuanian Literature and Art Archive, Vilnius.

Lithuanian Echo (*Lietuvos aidas*): in September 1932, she played Bach, Beethoven, Brahms, and her own *Capriccio*; and in January 1934, the Tchaikovsky *Violin Concerto* was her vehicle.[39] Her talents were considerable, and her technical abilities were appreciated.

Bacewicz began her 1935 *Trio for Oboe, Violin and Cello* in Paris and completed it in Warsaw. It was first performed in March 1936 by the great Polish oboist Seweryn Śnieckowski (1892–1958) in a promotional concert of contemporary chamber music organised by the Polish Music Publishing Society at the Warsaw Conservatory. The three-movement work was appreciated enthusiastically by both the audience and two Warsaw reviewers; it also won Second Prize (no First was awarded) by the Polish Music Publishers Society.

Composers frequently write from a connection with a player, and Bacewicz dedicated her 1936 *Sonata for Oboe and Piano* to Śnieckowski. The music ranges through grotesque, pensive, and joyous moments. It starts with a typical sonata-form movement, contrasting rhythmic and tuneful ideas, with a recurring, rondo-like main theme; there is a playful, wry humour. The dancing second movement, Tempo di Valse, is like a little barrel organ waltz – ethereal, fleeting, delicate, fading away at the end, as if something has been left unsaid. The third movement, Vivace, is buoyant, cheerful and amusing, with short sighs and modest cadenzas, the second of which launches the virtuosic finale.

In March 1935, Bacewicz entered the first Wieniawski International Violin Competition in Warsaw, an event organised by the nephew of Henryk Wieniawski (1835–80) to commemorate the 100th anniversary of the Polish violinist and composer's birth.[40] There was a strong line-up of competitors, and the fifteen-year-old Ginette Neveu won First Prize; Bacewicz received Honourable Mention to David Oistrakh's Second Place.[41] She became friends with Oistrakh and later wrote a story entitled 'King David', in which she – after watching Oistrakh teach a young French woman, using all his 'wisdom and goodness' – told of the thoughtful instruction method he had developed. She described how carefully he put the student at ease before saying, 'I did notice a few flaws.'[42]

Bacewicz recounted what happened in the Wieniawski Competition in her short story 'Bad Luck'. She had done so well in the first round that she was expected to win, and was due to play movements from Wieniawski's *Violin*

---

[39] See reviews in 'Bacewicz – First Successes', *Polmic.pl*.

[40] See '1st International Henryk Wieniawski Violin Competition, Warsaw, 3–16 March 1935': https://wieniawski.com/1ivc.html.

[41] David Oistrakh (1908–74) was a celebrated Soviet violinist and conductor.

[42] Bacewicz, 'King David', *Distinguishing Mark*, p. 75.

Concerto No. 2 in D minor in the second round. However, the day before round two, they had come home to find there had been a robbery at their Długa Street lodgings; much was stolen. They spent the night at the police station, and so Bacewicz didn't play as well as she could have the next day. She later said she thought the thief was an art-lover, considering what was left in their flat: a dress, shoes, and the violin.[43]

Marriage *'Z Ogniem'* (With Fire)

While in Warsaw, Bacewicz wrote her *Sinfonietta* for string orchestra (1935), which was premièred by the Polish Radio Orchestra in 1936. It received an honourable mention in a competition run by the Society for the Publication of Polish Music. Many of her hallmarks are present in this work: a sturdy, well-paced opening Allegro; a lyrical, dark-hued central Andante; and a finale which includes engaging surprises, such as the music frequently cutting across its 3/4 time signature.

It was around this time that Bacewicz first encountered her future husband, Andrzej Biernacki (1903–63); she was twenty-six, and he, thirty-two. They were introduced by his best friend, Bohdan Łosakiewicz, who played second violin in Bacewicz's string quartet group. A quiet, decisive man, Biernacki was a successful doctor for whom medicine was a vocation. In 1925, he was in Paris on an internship at the Louis Pasteur Institute and later, in 1928, undertook scientific work in Brazil. He won a scholarship to study in Vienna from the late autumn of 1935, and just before Christmas of that year, he moved on to the Carlo Forlanini Institute in Rome. Biernacki wrote from Rome in November 1935: 'My dearest Grażyna, I am again in a foreign country, among strangers. If I didn't have you or feel that you are always by my side, I would run away from this drifting.'[44] Bacewicz wrote to him – also in November 1935 – about a violin concert:

> My beloved, My Dearest Dudus!!! You forgot to take the stage fright/jitters with you away from me, and so I was terrified of going out. When I am as tired as now, I am always most afraid of not remembering things correctly. I have never had it before. Well fortunately it went all right. There were heaps of people there. I was terribly sorry you weren't there. I was thinking about you all the time. Wanda was over the moon that, according to her, I made such progress and she was sorry you couldn't be the witness of my success.[45]

Even though friends warned Bacewicz that Biernacki came from a traditional family and might expect her to become the same as his more conventional

---

[43] Ibid., p. 59.
[44] Biernacki cited in J. Sendłak, *Z Ogniem* (Warsaw: Skarpa Warzawska, 2018), p. 38.
[45] Ibid.

mother, the couple seem to have been devoted to one another, as the following letter from Biernacki reveals: 'Once I couldn't sleep and I started to remember all our earlier encounters. For example, the evening at Adria,[46] I noted that your steps are surprisingly big for a woman. Or during concerts when I was always meeting you with B. and I remember your very decisive, masculine handshake.'[47]

They fell in love, and both wanted to start a family. However, they were pulling in different directions; she had wanted to marry before he left on his scholarship abroad (probably because of the prevailing attitude that people were more respectful to married women).[48] She knew that his family would expect children soon after the marriage. Biernacki asked her to wait until he got back, and her friends advised her to agree to this. Wanda, especially, was worried about Bacewicz being overworked, undernourished, and upset about the separation. She played the violin in the day, in her string quartet group in the evenings, and wrote music at night. Wanda used to find her still composing at 3 am, totally focussed and in her own world. Bacewicz said she never felt tired when composing; she was full of energy and wanted to write down the sounds in her mind as quickly as possible.

Biernacki's scholarship took him to study in Vienna, Paris, Rome, Davos, then back to Paris and Berlin, and he returned to Poland in the autumn of 1936. The couple's frequent letters include this one from Bacewicz, dated 3 March 1936: 'You see, I am a woman of no limits. Just as my love to you knows no limits, I easily fall into despair because of you, generally everything in my life is out of proportion. I hope you will cure me of it all – except from my love to you, naturally.' Biernacki replied on 6 March from Rome: 'Our life together is most important to me. Do I take it easily? Wouldn't I prefer to go back? Grażyna, dearest, I never felt such longing in my life . . . Is it all worth it? Why all this suffering? I am in ever increasing frenzy.'[49] Without her by his side, life felt hollow for him: he wanted them to live their lives '*Z Ogniem*' (*With Fire*) – the title of the book about them by their granddaughter, Joanna Sendłak (b. 1966). Soon after his return to Warsaw, Bacewicz married Biernacki in a church wedding on 6 September 1936.[50] As described by Bacewicz, her husband was a practical and responsible person. Wanda also accounted for their days: mornings were allocated to work, and the afternoons were social fun – 'a little madness'.[51]

---

[46] A famous Polish night club for Warsaw's upper-middle class.

[47] Sendłak, *Z Ogniem*, p. 11. 'B' refers to Bohdan Łosakiewicz, Biernacki's roommate, and second violin in Bacewicz's Quartet.

[48] See Bacewicz, 'If I Were Single', *A Distinguishing Mark*, p. 77.

[49] Both letters in Sendłak, *Z Ogniem*, p. 321.

[50] According to Wanda, Biernacki lived with them as Bacewicz's fiancé some time before they married. Wanda Bacewicz in *Grażyna Bacewicz* (film), 1999; and Gąsiorowska, *Bacewicz*, p. 140.

[51] Wanda Bacewicz in *Bacewicz* (film), 1999.

Figure 7 Grzegorz Fitelberg

Polish Radio Orchestra

One significant friend for Bacewicz at this time was the Polish conductor, violinist, and composer Grzegorz Fitelberg (1879–1953). Fitelberg made a major contribution to Polish musical life, regularly promoting new music, and he was the chief conductor of the Warsaw Philharmonic Orchestra in 1923–35.

In 1935, Fitelberg helped to found the Polish National Radio Symphony Orchestra (PNRSO), inviting the most gifted instrumentalists to join. Bacewicz accepted the position of principal violinist and worked with them in this role for two years (1936–8). Leading the PNRSO helped her to understand orchestration, and the position also gave opportunities for her own works to be performed. Her sly, perky, and playful *Violin Concerto No. 1* may have come from this, and she premiered it with the Radio Orchestra in 1938. The work starts with the soloist giving a quasi-improvisatory display, joined by the orchestra in a skittish mood. The Andante is lyrical and wistful, interrupted towards the end by an eerie passage of string harmonics combined with high woodwind. The finale plays with 6/8 and 2/4 metres, and has her characteristic joie de vivre. However, she was not very happy with the piece. Bacewicz herself never spoke about her first violin concerto; but, recalling conversations with her sister, Wanda confirmed her aversion to the piece.[52]

---

[52] Ibid.

Bacewicz was a severe critic of her own work. Although she had already written two string quartets by the mid-1930s, she remained dissatisfied with them, and only recognised the string quartet she composed in 1938 as 'No. 1'. It was premiered in Paris in April 1939 by a quartet led by the Puerto Rican violinist José Figueroa (1905–98), whom Bacewicz had met during her studies with Boulanger. One of her first major works, it is tuneful and light in tone; perhaps naming the work 'Number 1' suggests confidence in its achievement. In the neoclassical vein, this quartet also demonstrates her understanding of string sonority and practices. She begins with a classical exposition and then has a free recapitulation, rather than a conventional return. The lyrical Andante tranquillo builds five variations on the demure Lithuanian folksong 'Vai żydėk, żydėk', which invites a dry, leafless apple tree to flower. The jaunty finale has folkdance associations; nominally in 2/4, she often cuts across the metre with teasing ingenuity, wrong-footing the listener.

The year 1938 was also the year in which Bacewicz completed her first symphony. Possibly in another bout of self-criticism, she did not include this piece in her official list of works – it remains unpublished – but the work highlights the time as a significant step in her composing. The opening movement is gritty, disjointed, and rhythmically driven and is followed by a yearning, anguished Adagio. Then comes a scurrying Allegretto, with a Theme and Variations to finish.

In January 1939, Bacewicz returned to Paris to help with preparations for a concert of her own works, given on 26 April at the École Normale de Musique. Along with the premiere of *String Quartet No. 1* (1938), the concert included her *Oboe Trio* (1935) and *Oboe Sonata* (1936), which were performed by notable artists such as the oboist Louis Bleuzet (1884–1941), professor at the Paris Conservatoire, and the Puerto Rican brothers of the Figueroa Quartet (José, Jaime, Guillermo, and Rafael). She returned to Poland two months before the outbreak of World War II.

World War II

Nazi Germany was becoming increasingly aggressive at this time; and in August 1939, Poland was divided into Nazi- and Soviet-controlled zones. Hitler invaded in September 1939, and Warsaw fell on 27 September. Hans Frank (1900–46) was appointed Governor-General of occupied Poland, over-seeing the persecution of the Jews. Attempting to wipe out Poland as a nation, the Nazis degraded society by exterminating certain groups through the elimin-ation of education, closing performance venues, and banning the arts in general. Following almost five years of German occupation, the Warsaw Uprising of

August 1944 tried to free the city. However, Warsaw was obliterated in October (1944) – the Nazis blew it up as they left. Nearly 90 per cent of the buildings were destroyed by January 1945. In turn, the Soviets also strove to wreck Polish culture, with a similar policy of repression.

During the years that Poland was under German rule (1939–44), authorities required mandatory registration of all musicians, and music that was performed in public had to be approved in advance by the German office. Musical life in Poland was, therefore, greatly restricted. Cultural activities did continue illegally, but music was forced into a clandestine existence. The musicians remaining in Poland banded together to fight for Polish music, and Bacewicz became a member of the secret Underground Musicians' Union (established in Warsaw in 1939). The Union worked closely with the Polish Resistance Movement, fighting to retain the dignity of Polish artists. Avoiding the compulsory registration, Bacewicz and other members of the Union organised secret concerts, performing music that was forbidden by the Germans; many concerts were held at the Home of Art Café (*Dom Sztuki*), organised by the composer Bolesław Woytowicz (1899–1980). Out of concern for the safety of the participants, the programmes were rarely conceived in advance: a list of artists and addresses was never available. Bacewicz also gave concerts for the Commission for Polish Relief, an organisation that distributed additional rations that were provided by Allies. She appeared in these secret concerts and at the concerts of the Main Guardianship Council (*Rada Główna Opiekuńcza*), giving financial support to musicians who were usually unemployed.

Scared of the bombing and working hard to manage her feelings, Bacewicz developed a nervous trembling in her body, which perhaps reflected her awareness of the trouble to come.[53] In 1939, a bomb landed right outside their house at ul. Koszykowa 35 but didn't explode. After the first bombardments, she and her family left the city and (with much of the population) walked the nearly forty miles south-eastward to reach Garwolin. In the barracks there, as they began to eat, Bacewicz suddenly began to shudder and said, 'Let's get out of here. We have to leave right now!'[54] After she had got her family across the bridge, they saw the bombers – and then Garwolin ceased to exist.

The family went next towards Lublin, and, after meeting various adventures on the way, reached Marynin (about eleven kilometres west of Lublin), where they stayed in the house of Biernacki's family. The family eventually returned to Warsaw, where Bacewicz composed and gave underground concerts. At this time, her home in ul. Koszykowa 35 was often an oasis for the continuation of

---

[53] Described in her story 'Right Before Our Eyes', *A Distinguishing Mark*, p. 45.
[54] Ibid., p. 46.

Polish culture, with Bacewicz's musical friends, including Lutosławski, Sikorski, and Witold Rudziński (Director of the Warsaw Philharmonic, 1948–49), coming round. Stefan Kisielewski recalled years later:

> I spent many, many hours during the occupation at the Biernackis in ul. Koszykowa [Warsaw]. It was a welcoming and warm home; it provided such an excellent relief from the horror, sadness, despair and all other repulsive things brought to Warsaw by the Germans. And how much one ate and, especially drank there . . . oh my! Interestingly, although I was there often, I didn't talk much with Grażyna about music, about composing. She didn't like to express her musical feelings much; very delicate towards the others, she also jealously guarded the secrets of her work, her evolutions and transformations.[55]

While in Warsaw, Bacewicz gave birth to a daughter, Alina Biernacka, on 30 September 1942. A few years later Bacewicz wrote to her brother, Vytautas: 'In respect to my child I am very patient (Andrzej says too patient) and completely compliant. I approach her only with love and am bringing her up on love. There's no question of using any force with Alinka and actually I listen to her, and not the other way around. Despite this, results are very good.'[56] Carrying on the family's creative traditions, Alina became a successful poet.

Compositions during the War

Bacewicz continued to write music throughout World War II. Her *Three Preludes* for piano date from 1941, as does the unaccompanied *Violin Sonata No. 1*. This four-movement sonata owes much to the Bach solo partitas and sonatas, combined with her own original ideas. There are ostinatos and figurations, lyrical ideas, and instrumental devices such as double stops and open-string drones/pedal points. She also composed a *Symphony No. 1* (this one *with* a number on it) between 1942 and 1945, and the work was first performed on 28 May 1948 in Kraków.

Her *String Quartet No. 2* (1942) was first performed in May 1943 at an underground concert in Bolesław Woytowicz's Art Café.[57] The quartet group was led by one of the foremost Polish violinists of the time, Eugenia Umińska (1910–80), and included Tadeusz Ochlewski (1894–1975), the future head of the post-war Polish Music Publishing, PWM, on second violin. Even with its

---

[55] S. Kisielewski, 'Grażyna Bacewicz i jej czasy' (Kraków: PWM, 1964), p. 12.

[56] Bacewicz's letter to Vytautas (30 August 1947), in *From Notes and Letters of Grazyna Bacewicz*, ed. W. Bacewicz, trans. W. Wilk, *Polish Music. Center*: https://polishmusic.usc.edu/research/ publications/polish-music-journal/vol1no2/grazyna-bacewicz-notes-and-letters/#1

[57] See 'Bacewicz, 'War and the First Post-War Years', *Polmic.pl*: https://bacewicz.polmic.pl/en/ war-and-the-first-post-war-years.

origins in the war's difficult circumstances, this quartet includes moments of repose, and a sense of grief and nostalgia; the viola has a particular role, with solos in the first and third movements. Some Bacewicz fingerprints emerge, such as sighing glissandos and haunted rocking motifs, in the middle of the slow movement, which is also connected to Polish folk music. With its wartime context, this second, tougher quartet is contrapuntally dense, with a dark harmonic and textural palette – even in the finale, which, for Bacewicz, was conventionally the release.

The *Suite for Two Violins* was also written in 1943 and premiered at one of the underground concerts by Umińska and Irena Dubiska (1899–1989). There are seven well-contrasted movements in this work, made of inventive dialogue. The opening Allegro is march-like, and a flowing 9/8 Andante follows. Next comes a playful 6/8 Vivo, and after an elegant Minuet, energy returns in a forthright Allegro; the sixth movement is an Andante Fughetta, with a brilliant Allegro to finish. In this work, Bacewicz combines simple, baroque gestures with harsh harmonies, occasionally coloured by chromaticism.

Rootless Wanderings and an *Overture*

Bacewicz remained in Warsaw for most of World War II at a time when all professional careers would have been difficult. Following the Warsaw Uprising in August 1944, however, and the wounding of her younger sister, Wanda, the family decided to flee their home. Due to the rushed escape, manuscripts of Bacewicz's works would have been left behind in their house – if it hadn't been for a friend who rescued them; however, their home was one of few houses to escape the fire storm of Nazi destruction.

Figure 8 Warsaw 1945

Fleeing Warsaw, the family first went to a camp in Pruszków, and then they took Wanda to a hospital in Grodzisk Masowiecki (about thirty kilometres south-west of Warsaw). Here, Bacewicz gave some music lessons and looked after her mother, her two-year-old daughter, and her sister, Wanda, while Biernacki organised a ward of Warsaw's Infant Jesus Hospital, which had been evacuated to Grodzisk Mazowiecki.[58] In 1945, they relocated briefly to Lublin, where Bacewicz gave a concert with Keijstut, playing Tartini, Mozart, Szymanowski, and her own works; but the family returned to Warsaw only after the end of the war.[59] Wanda described all these moves as a somewhat rootless wandering.

Bacewicz completed her symphonic *Overture* in 1943, and the piece was eventually premiered at the first Festival of Polish Music held in Kraków on 1 September 1945. One of her most popular pieces, it has great energy, celebratory themes, and colourful use of brass and percussion. Its robust, rhythmic drive starts with the pulsing motif from the opening of Beethoven's *Fifth Symphony* (representing the letter 'V' in Morse code) that the BBC borrowed as its wartime Victory call signal. Then the brass instruments interject short descending staccato stabs. An Andante section blends cello, horns, and woodwinds. Chaotic energy returns, with trumpets and horns proclaiming a fanfare and building to a powerful end. Even at this time, her energetic manner and unconventional orchestration suggest confidence and optimism.

Aftermath

Poland paid a dreadful price for World War II: images of Auschwitz and the Warsaw Ghetto continue to be vivid in people's minds. It is still difficult today to grasp a true picture of the tragedy, but it is thought that up to 20 per cent of Poland's population died as a result of the occupation.[60] This also produced a sense of suffering; Poles tried to alleviate the feeling through works of pent-up emotion. The *Tragic Overture* (1942) of Bacewicz's younger colleague, Andrzej Panufnik (1914–91), was written in the mood of dread in Nazi-occupied Warsaw 'under

---

[58] Ibid.

[59] Bacewicz's story 'An Understanding' (*A Distinguishing Mark*, pp. 51–2) describes the Lublin concert. The temperature was so cold she stopped playing. They went off to get overcoats, and the audience applauded loudly on their return. After the bravos, there was stamping of feet: the listeners also needed to get warm.

[60] See Adam Easton, 'Poland still counts losses from WW2', BBC News website (31 August 2019): www.bbc.co.uk/news/world-europe-49523932.

the influence of the fear and horror of our daily lives'.[61] However, bringing up a young daughter, nursing her sister, and helping her husband in his work in these circumstances didn't stop Bacewicz from finding time to practice the violin during these years. In 1946, she appeared as the soloist with the Orchestre des Concerts Lamoureux in Szymanowski's *Violin Concerto No. 1* at the Salle Pleyel in Paris. It is a masterpiece of orchestral writing, and Szymanowski's ideas also influenced her when she came to write her own *Violin Concerto No. 3* in 1948.

Immediately after the war, people in Poland were hungry for all forms of culture and, despite limited opportunities, they started to rebuild the old infrastructures. Łódź was important, as it had remained intact. Bacewicz's musical alma mater, the original Music Conservatory in Łódź started by Helena Kijeńska-Dobkiewicz, was revived in April 1945 as the State Conservatory of Music. Out of local pride, it was renamed the Grażyna and Kiejstut Bacewicz Academy of Music in 1999.

2 After the War: 1945–54

The re-establishment of Europe's war-torn nations was discussed at the Yalta Conference (February 1945), which considered the post-war reorganisation of Germany and Europe. Poland was the first item on the Soviet agenda; since Russia had sinned against Poland, Stalin said that they should atone for their offences. The Soviet Union allowed for a coalition government composed of the communists, including the Polish Workers' Party; so, a communist government was installed. Warsaw was a city of rubble, its artistic organisations in disarray. After this disruption, revival was essential: there was the need both for housing and to recover their self-respect. The Polish people rebuilt the city, with support from the Soviet Union. Warsaw's residents recycled the city's rubble in the reconstruction. Twenty-two street scenes by the eighteenth-century artist Bernardo Bellotto (1721–80) were used as blueprints.[62]

---

[61] Panufnik, note to *Tragic Overture*, Boosey & Hawkes: www.boosey.com/cr/music/Andrzej-Panufnik-Tragic-Overture/7643.

[62] Bellotto was the court painter to the King of Poland from 1768 and, somehow, his paintings survived the war: they were confiscated by the Germans, kept in various castles, and finally returned to the Warsaw National Museum in 1946. See Philip McCouat, 'Bernardo Bellotto and the Reconstruction of Warsaw', *Journal of Art in Society*: www.artinsociety.com/bernardo-bellotto-and-the-reconstruction-of-warsaw.html.

In 1945–6, Bacewicz worked as a professor in the Helena Kijeńska-Dobkiewicz Conservatory (renamed the State Conservatory of Music in March 1945) in Łódź. Notwithstanding the difficult situation, 1945 was a busy year for her and she completed eleven works; these included *Symphony No. 1, Easy Duets on Folk Themes; Legenda* for violin and piano*; Sonata da camera; Scherzo* for violin*; Concertino for Violin and Piano (in first and third positions); Farfarello* (musical accompaniment to a radio play based on *Róża* by Stefan Żeromski), and *O Janku co psom szyl buty* (another radio play, on a children's rhyme about a dog who made shoes). She composed the virtuosic *Violin Concerto No. 2* in 1945–6. The particularly beautiful slow movement's sensuous melody is a kind of sweet lament with blue notes. She was the soloist at the première on 18 October 1946, with the Łódź Philharmonic Orchestra.

Violin teaching in Łódź was probably the reason for writing the *Easy Duets on Folk Themes* (1945, two violins) and the *Concertino in first and third position*. Suitable for students, the latter has two fast movements sandwiching a tuneful *Romance*.[63] Her series of five sonatas for violin and piano (1945–51) were a major contribution to the repertoire. The first, a vigorous *Sonata da camera* (1945), re-creates a baroque suite, referring to the florid manner of the eighteenth century. The stately opening Largo is followed by Allegro, with the composer's own version of classical figuration. A graceful minuet has baroque-style mordents in the piano; then a heartfelt Andante sostenuto; and finally an amusingly playful Gigue – Molto Allegro.

Her brother Vytautus had been on tour in Argentina when the Germans occupied Lithuania, rendering him an exile. He expressed his feeling about the war in his *Symphony No. 2*, named 'de la Guerra' (1940), and dedicated it to Grażyna.[64] From that year he settled in America, teaching and composing. Due to the siblings' geographical separation, he was the family member with whom Grażyna had the most written correspondence.[65] Grażyna's letter of

---

[63] Bacewicz, *Concertino for Violin and Piano (in 1ˢᵗ–3ʳᵈ positions)*, PWM Edition: https://pwm.com.pl/en/sklep/publikacja/concertino,grazyna-bacewicz,1264,shop.html.

[64] In 2007, Toccata Classics issued a CD of Vytautas Bacevičius's orchestral music, performed by the Lithuanian State Symphony Orchestra, which includes his *Symphony No. 2*: https://toccata classics.com/product/bacevicius-orchestral-music.

[65] See Malgorzata Janicka-Slysz (ed.), trans. Jan Rybicki, 'The Letters of Grażyna Bacewicz and Vytautas Bacevičius, (1945–1969; part I)': www.gkr.uni-leipzig.de/fileadmin/Fakult%C3%A4t_GKO/Musikwissenschaft/2.2-Forschung/Musikerbriefe/18_1_JanSly1.pdf.

20 August 1945 to her brother gives a vivid description of the wreckage of Warsaw and her musical activities:

Dear Vitek:

We were so happy when, on 20th August, 1945, we finally received two letters from you … We see from your letters, however, that you have no idea at all what we've gone through and how much we've had to endure. You write about bombardments in Warsaw as if that had been the only threat. Suffice to say that Warsaw is no more, that the city is gone but for a few houses, that there is no railway station there, not a single bridge, nothing but heaps of ruins. Don't get me wrong: I'm not exaggerating.

You must have heard of the uprising in Warsaw, of how we fought Germans with little more than our bare hands, of how the Germans slaughtered the populace etc., etc. Mummy's house does not exist, it has burnt down with Wandzia's whole library and everything, so has Kiejstut's – they have also lost everything. Our house seems to be all right (in fact, our side-wing is standing but the front part is collapsed), but it's been looted …

My recent feats include music for a play (for the money) and my Overture will be performed at a festival in Kraków in a couple of days. I go to Kraków a lot, and to Warsaw too … to play concerts … Let me tell you a funny thing, too. I'm doing literature as well now. A short story of mine was read on the Radio yesterday. I've already written a novel and a half and some smaller texts as well …

So here we are in Łódź (we still live in a hotel since we can't find an apartment) …

I'm in good form, violin-wise. I don't think I've ever played so well. I'm finishing my Second Violin Concerto. Your letter arrived by the same post with one from Father (from Lithuania). He's alive and well, at the same address. He's working as before. Make sure you write as much as you can.

Love Grażyna[66]

Warsaw was destroyed; recovery was painful, with the oppressive cultural doctrine and the resentment of the liberation by the Red Army. Despite these complications, Bacewicz kept composing, continuing in her personal way, withstanding pressure and maintaining her integrity.[67] Eventually, Bacewicz and Biernacki went back to their Warsaw flat in Koszykowa Street.

---

[66] Bacewicz (20 August 1945) in ibid., pp. 1–2.

[67] After a tirade in 1936 in *Pravda* entitled 'Muddle instead of Music' about his opera *Lady Macbeth of Mtsensk*, Shostakovich had a difficult relationship with the government of the Soviet Union.

Figure 9 Residence: Koszykowa St 35 building

Music behind the 'Iron Curtain'

On 5 March 1946 in the USA, Winston Churchill delivered his 'Iron Curtain' speech, noting the political domination of the USSR and the perceived threat to the Eastern Bloc.[68] As a result, artists in Poland became subject to the USSR's policy of socialist realism – the diktat that sought to use art for political purposes. Izabela Pacewicz commented in 'Socialist Realism in Polish Music':

> Undoubtedly, the most negative effect was the final slam of 'the Iron Curtain'. Polish composers became cut off from the avant-garde current of European music … there were no direct contacts with their colleagues from the West or an opportunity to listen to their works, but even of getting to know their scores,

---

[68] See, for example, 'Winston Churchill Warns of Soviet "Iron Curtain"', *New York Times* (5 March 2012): https://learning.blogs.nytimes.com/2012/03/05/march-5-1946-winston-churchill-warns-of-soviet-iron-curtain.

which were subject to the censor's confiscation. Because of this, composers focused on the possibilities that existed within the current political rules.[69]

Observing further, Daniel Elphick has noted that:

As part of the new Soviet domination over Poland, the aesthetic [socialist realism] was forced upon Polish artists, though to varying degrees of success. The artistic climate in Poland demanded alterations and adjustments to the Soviet scheme of socialist realism, which resulted in a distinctly Polish variant called *socrealizm*.[70]

In October 1946, the Soviet Composers Union assembly addressed the beginnings of an artistic crackdown. Resolutions included the need for 'more creative guidance' and 'closer ties between Soviet composers and Soviet reality'.[71] There were increasing calls for nationalism and unity in Polish music, and Bacewicz continued both composing and performing, with considerable exposure in Polish musical life immediately after the War. Her works were regularly performed by the Polish Radio Orchestra, the National Philharmonic Orchestra, and others; these organisations commissioned compositions, helped by the socialist Culture Office's programme of financial support.

The music Bacewicz wrote in 1946 included the *Violin Sonata No. 2*, the *Capriccio* for violin and piano, *Suite for Strings,* and *From Old Music* for small orchestral ensemble. The *Violin Sonata No. 2* opens with an Allegro that balances strength and subtlety. The Andante contrasts poignancy with some grandiosity. Then comes a bright, rhythmic Scherzo, and finally, a muscular, slightly declamatory Allegro molto. Her *String Quartet No. 3* was composed during a concert tour of France (1947) and was later recognised by the Polish Ministry of Culture and Art Awards of 1955.[72] An admirer of the work, Lutosławski said that this quartet was 'marked by an exceptional polyphonic skill in addition to its masterly idiomatic writing for string quartet'.[73] Bacewicz's biographer Małgorzata Gąsiorowska called it her most important work of 1947.

What would musical life have been like for Bacewicz under state control? Cut off from developments in the West, yet more liberal than other Eastern bloc states, the

---

[69] Izabela Pacewicz, 'Social Realism in Polish Music', in Marek Podhajski (ed.), *Polish Music: Polish Composers 1918–2010* (Gdansk & Lublin: Publishing House of John Paul II Catholic University of Lublin, 2013), p. 189.

[70] Daniel Elphick, *Music behind the Iron Curtain: Weinberg and His Polish Contemporaries* (Cambridge: Cambridge University Press, 2019), p. 88.

[71] Ibid., p. 98. Bacewicz's Polish colleague, Mieczysław Weinberg (1919–96), the subject of Elphick's book, suffered Jewish persecution and fled to Russia at the outbreak of World War II. His compositional output was prolific, including seventeen string quartets and twenty-six symphonies.

[72] For further details about this piece, see 'Bacewicz, *String Quartet No. 3*', *Polmic.pl*: https://bacewicz.polmic.pl/en/string-quartet-no-3.

[73] Lutoslawski, 'Foreword' in Rosen, *Grażyna Bacewicz*.

Polish People's Republic was a puppet entity controlled by the Soviet Union, although Stalinism permeated society less than in neighbouring countries. From 1945 to 1954, he imposed the socialist realist doctrine (which was not realistic at all) by relying on media control and an army of secret police. Party policy approved what was 'understandable'. Sometimes labelled formalist (meaning out-of-touch), dissonant, or atonal, 'modern' music was censured for not being easily understood.[74] In the doctrine of socialist realism in the arts, the government demanded an overt connection to the experiences of the masses – in a simplified language, often using folk tunes, and ending optimistically.[75] As in other European socialist countries after the War, artistic institutions in Poland were nationalised. Philharmonic societies, symphony orchestras and music schools were created to popularise Polish art. The government's publishing house, Polskie Wydawnictwo Muzyczne (PWM), was founded in 1945.[76]

Despite increasing state intervention, 1947–9 were among the most productive years of Bacewicz's career. The Union of Polish Composers was established at the National Congress of Polish Composers (Kraków, 1945), and Bacewicz became a member, and later vice-president. The fact that she was a woman did not appear to hinder her career. Under state socialism, gender equality was a principle, but not a right; theory and practice diverged. Apparently, Bacewicz simply got on with what she wanted to do. She did, however, receive frequent correspondence addressed to *Mr.* Bacewicz; one of her stories relates that she often received communications to 'Dear Mister Grażyna Bacewicz'.[77] Additionally, after a performance of her 1949 *Piano Concerto* in Vienna, a music critic wrote that it was a 'known fact that in the shadow of Grażyna Bacewicz stands a man who writes her compositions for her'.[78] Such irritating lies and misconceptions did not deter her from writing and performing music.

The Polish Ministry of Culture and Art

Shortly after the war had ended, the Polish Ministry of Culture and Art (MKiS) took on the role of state sponsor or underwriter. Through the years 1949–55, the state

---

[74] For a detailed consideration of socialist realism in Russia, see Andrey Olkhovsky, *Music Under the Soviets: The Agony of an Art* (New York: Praeger Publications, 1955).

[75] See also Adrian Thomas's note on *Violin Concerto No. 4* in the CD booklet accompanying 'Grażyna Bacewicz Violin Concertos Nos, 2, 4 & 5' (Chandos Records Ltd., CHAN 10673, 2011), p. 6.

[76] For further details, see Teresa Chylinska, 'Polskie Wydawnictwo Muzyczne [PWM; Polish Music Publications]', *Grove Music Online*: www.oxfordmusiconline.com/grovemusic/view/10 .1093/gmo/9781561592630.001.0001/omo-9781561592630-e-0000022039.

[77] Bacewicz, *A Distinguishing Mark*, p. 27.

[78] Cited in Wanda Walk, 'An Outline History of Women Composers in Poland', Polish Music Center: https://polishmusic.usc.edu/research/publications/essays/wilk-wanda-history-of-women-composers.

provided material help and cultural patronage, rebuilding musical institutions and enforcing socialist realism. With the Ministry directing cultural policy, these were awkward times. Jointly with the Composers Union, the Ministry created the Commission for Commissions and Purchases. Bacewicz's story 'A Discovery' describes the practical process by which the Ministry calculated the fees: multiplying the length of the composition (minutes) by the number of people performing it.[79]

Music helped the Communist party to establish legitimacy, and Poland's rulers sought to fill public spaces with the production of music. In August 1949, the MKiS organised a conference in Łagów, at which the implementation of socialist realism in Polish music was debated. According to Adrian Thomas, one of the ideas to emerge from the conference was the setting up of a new Festival of Polish Music, and the MKiS established a special grant fund to encourage composers to write new pieces for this festival.[80] It had two intentions: to celebrate the music of the People's Republic of Poland, and to be a port of call in the overriding cultural and political issue of the time – developing socialist realism. But there was a confusing contradiction in music: composers were seen as influential while, creatively, their individualism was seen as a threat to socialist society.

The Festival was to have a special emphasis on contemporary music, and in March 1950, a letter was sent by the Polish Composers' Union (on behalf of MKiS) to Polish composers inviting them to submit compositions for the performance at the Festival. Bacewicz submitted her *Polish Dance Suite* (*Cykl tancow polskich*), an unnamed ballet, and a *Cello Concerto*. She was awarded a grant totalling 240,000 zloti for several compositions (over £4,600 at the historical exchange rate).[81] Because of the low fees that the Ministry paid, however, composers had to find other means of remuneration. Managing these political restrictions, Lutosławski earned a living by composing utilitarian works for schools and the radio – they named a studio after him[82] – and Panufnik conducted two of the principal orchestras.[83]

Wanda described this time of socialist realism as a 'tragedy' and a period of 'nervous breakdown'; most composers resisted it.[84] Bacewicz was a highly respected artist and one of the few Polish composers who were successful in accommodating the orthodoxy in her music: without providing propaganda, she wrote in ways that could be politically justified. Her use of traditional forms and

---

[79] Bacewicz, 'A Discovery', *A Distinguishing Mark*, p. 90.

[80] For full details, see Adrian Thomas, 'File 750: "Composers, Politics, and the Festival of Polish Music (1951)"', *On Polish Music and Other Topics*: https://onpolishmusic.com/articles/•-file-750-2002.

[81] Ibid.

[82] See 'Witold Lutoslawski Concert Studio of Polish Radio', *Polskie Radio*: www2.polskieradio.pl /studio/lutoslawski_en.aspx.

[83] See 'Andrzej Panufnik', *Culture.pl*: https://culture.pl/en/artist /andrzej-panufnik.

[84] Wanda Bacewicz in *Grażyna Bacewicz* (film), 1999.

genres as well as folk idioms helped her to avoid censure, and many of her best known and enduring works date from this period. Though *socrealizm* lasted from 1949 to 1954, Bacewicz wrote extensively in her usual sphere during this time, producing forty-seven instrumental works.

Paris

It should be noted that prior to MKiS's Festival of Polish Music, Bacewicz had enjoyed considerable success as a composer-performer outside Polish borders. 'La musique Polonaise sous l'occupation' was the title of a chamber music concert she performed at the Salle des Concerts du Conservatoire, Paris, in April 1946.[85] The works performed had been composed during the war and included her *Suite* for two violins. On 23 May 1946, she gave a recital at the Salle Gaveau, where she played her own *Sonata da Camera* and works which still feature in violin recitals: *Prelude & Allegro* by Pugnani-Kreisler, *Caprice* by Paganini-Szymanowski, Wieniawski's *Scherzo Taratanella*, and Lili Boulanger's *Nocturne*. On this fifth Paris visit, she also performed Szymanowski's *Violin Concerto No. 1* with the Orchestre des Concerts Lamoureux, conducted by Paul Kletzki (1900–73), at the Salle Pleyel.[86] Writing to her brother, she started with the time it took to travel the nearly one thousand miles to Paris, and ended with concerns about her father in Lithuania:

Hotel Ramzès, 28 March 1946

Dear Vitek: I've been in Paris for a week. It took me six days to get here . . . I'm playing Szymanowski's Concerto No. 1 with Kletzki and Orchestra at the Salle Pleyel on May 9th. Kletzki is a Paris celebrity . . . and a marvellous conductor. Meanwhile, on April 27th, there's a chamber music concert at the Salle Gaveau with my Suite for Two Violins, even before that [I played a] recital mostly for the Polish colony here, and then a great recital in Lyon . . . What about you? . . . You wrote to me to buy your Sonata – OK, and what am I supposed to do with it? I don't think I quite got what you meant . . .

We're very worried for Father; we've heard there are mass deportations now from the Baltic States deep into Russia. Our letters come back undelivered, no news from him. How will this end? . . . Write to me as soon as possible.

Love, Grażyna[87]

---

[85] Rosen, *Grażyna Bacewicz*.

[86] See 'Paul Kletzki (Conductor)', Bach Cantatas website: www.bach-cantatas.com/Bio/Kletzki-Paul.html.

[87] Bacewicz (28 March 1946) in 'Letters of Grażyna Bacewicz and Vytautas Bacivičius (1945–1969)', pp. 2–3. Bacewicz here refers to rumours of mass deportations. Later, in the March 1949 deportations from the Baltic States, people were seized from their homes without warning and transported to the frozen ends of the Earth, a singularly low point in the Soviet Union's oppressive history. Some 100,000 Estonians, Latvians, and Lithuanians were sent to Siberia in cattle trucks to scratch a living from the permafrost in labour camps. Many died and only a few returned home. Evidently, their father survived, as he died in 1952.

Here is another letter of hers from Paris addressed to Vitek:

21 May 1946

Dear Brother: Kiejstut received some old letters by Father . . . He is now a school inspector, not a school manager anymore . . . This has calmed us down a bit, though the news is almost six months old now . . .

I'm playing hide-and-seek with the Embassy; that is, I pretend to be nice but I keep on going against the grain. I've ignored all their invitations to parties at the Embassy. They know I side with the reactionaries, but they can't turn and tell me to go to hell because I'm returning to Poland and could tell on them . . .

Write again! Grażyna[88]

With post-war Soviet dominance, caution was continually needed in communications to and from Poland:

Paris, 17 June 1946

Dearest Brother: I'm so sad we won't be able to write candidly any longer now that I'm going back to Poland. Try to be more circumspect when you write to me there. A musician has been arrested recently, a great friend of mine. He's still in jail . . . I wish you much success in all your plans and endeavours.

Love and kisses, Grażyna.
When do you think we will get to see you?[89]

Discretion and tactical advice feature in a different way in the next letter:

Paris, 20 November 1946

Dear Vitek:

I'm so sorry you're sad. Don't hate me for my 'wise' advice, but it seems so natural. Remember, Little Brother: an artist can only be looked up to by other people! If you keep on complaining to every Tom, Dick and Harry that you're being ignored, that you're in trouble, all you get is pity or thinly disguised joy. When you're down on your luck, don't tell even your closest friend. Don't forget you don't perform because you don't feel like it, not because you can't. Try to change your tactics, Brother. This is the first step to success. The second: get rid of your debts! This is essential! You're only getting further and further away from your goal if you keep on worrying about us. Why don't you try to concentrate on composing for a bit? They'll perform you once, then twice, then you'll play a Piano Concerto – perhaps a new one, not too heavy, nice-sounding, not too difficult – somewhere else, and things will start to happen . . .

Grażyna[90]

Polish families were always close. These siblings were devoted to each other, and she understood that her brother's somewhat eccentric, chaotic persona

---

[88] Ibid., p. 3.   [89] Ibid.   [90] Ibid., p. 4.

served him. Their correspondence shows that she is practical, almost parental, frank, and for all their differences, she expresses considerable concern.

Paris, 21 March 1947

Brother Dear ... Since you write so much about your work, let me say a few words about myself. You see, Polish composers have long freed themselves from Szymanowski's influence and have gone their various ways. I go my own way, for I pay most attention to form. I think that just as by piling stones one on another, with no plan, no order, one will never build a house and the pile will always crumble, there are some principles of construction in a work of music that must help it to stand. Of course, the laws don't need to be old, God forbid. Music can be either simpler or more complex, no matter ... but it must be well constructed. I don't even talk about good orchestration, because that goes without saying. I've thrown away my old pieces. Now that I know so much more than before I see their many weak points – so what is the point in keeping them? Sorry: I am not God, I don't see anything I do or write as final. Still, this does nothing to stop me from being happy that you are God ... You write that Preludes are trifles when compared to your great compositions. I know, but want the merest trifle to be flawless. And it's not the performance that makes or breaks a work ... Don't be so conceited with us; when we write to you, it's to help you, not to be a nuisance. If you feel offended by us, who in the world will be allowed to be candid with you?[91]

Probably they were brought up to be candid and unassuming. Later that year, she communicated her thoughts about playing the violin:

14 August 1947

Dear Vitek: ... I keep on wondering why on earth you should be so keen on the career of a virtuoso. This virtuoso thing is such a nuisance for me in my own life; if you want to know the truth, I would really prefer to be a composer and nothing more. I have the feeling that neither you nor I will ever become great virtuosi, simply because we're both too old and too vulnerable ... If you want to compose well, you have to concentrate on it ... In general, I think you're not on the right path: you have such a great gift of composition, yet, to tell you the truth, I think you're throwing it all away, worrying about things of lesser value than creativity. You thrash about like a lion in a cage, and where is this going to lead you? For obvious reasons, you cannot return to Poland or Lithuania ...

As for myself, if someone told me one day that I'm to stop being a violinist, I would be overjoyed. I play because it seems dishonourable to stop, by pure inertia, and also because that's what keeps me in money in Poland, but I really would rather earn less and care less, and sit at home, and stick to my composing. That's my dream. Yet when I'm in Paris, composing is out of the question (no place to do it); in Poland I'm thrown from one concert to another, so I can only compose in-

---

[91] Ibid., pp. 4–5.

between, at night. This is all wrong. But enough about me. It's you that I – and all of us – have at heart!'[92]

Given her substantial performing career, she is modest about her success. As a violinist she was admired for clear intonation, brilliant technique, and use of the entire palette of colours. In chamber concerts, her repertoire included music by Mozart, Mendelssohn, Tchaikovsky, Khachaturian, Prokofiev, and Szymanowski. Here is a posthumous tribute from her colleague, the Polish violinist Eugenia Umińska: 'Miss Bacewicz had amazing ease of technique, security and flexibility in both hands, unfailingly strong fingers, crystal clean intonation, firm and elastic rhythm, absolute security in organising interpretation and memory.'[93] Bacewicz's letter of 14 August 1947 (previously quoted) clearly illustrates that it was not so easy for her to 'stop being a violinist': after working with the instrument for many years, she said that it was like being married to it.

Folk Music and Abundant Classic Creations

Bacewicz found it equally difficult to stop being a composer, and her nation's rich tradition of folk music continued to be an important source of inspiration for her here. The rediscovery of traditional folk music was a factor in broadening the horizons of Western music; it gave music an audible national identity, a new tonal language coming from the folk and dance idioms. Both a conservative influence and a force for change, it contributed strength to Polish music. Chopin had made triple-time dance music popular (the mazurka and the polonaise); the duple-time krakowiak came from the south; and Podhale had a lively tradition. Szymanowski blended refined art with primitive folk music of the Polish highlands.[94]

Bacewicz absorbed folklore's characteristics. Polish folkdances were lively and joyful, and she was particularly fond of the athletic oberek. For her, traditional music was a rich source of inspiration; she absorbed the tone of folk material into her personal musical language, so it seemed like the indigenous element was in her blood. After the war, folklore became synonymous with nationalism, and so, collecting and categorising folk traditions began at this time. But, controlling artistic creativity, the doctrine of socialist realism was used to discriminate against works of art: Lutosławski's *Symphony No. 1* was

---

[92] Ibid., p. 5.

[93] Eugenia Umińska, 'A Memory of Grażyna Bacewicz', *Ruch Muzyczny* 7 (1969), p. 10.

[94] See Jim Samson, 'Szymanowski and Polish Nationalism', *The Musical Times*, vol. 131/1765 (March 1990), p. 137. Further details about Polish folk music and songs can also be found on the Polonia Music website: www.poloniamusic.com/Gorale_Podhale_HIghlander_Goralska_Kapela_Goralski_Music.html.

blacklisted for many years.[95] Like other composers, Bacewicz was subject to increasing ideological regulation by the socialist government. She worked around it, however, conscious of the political clouds looming over Poland. On a trip to Prague in 1948, she (again) cautioned Vitek about government editorial control, with respect to what he wrote:

Prague, 18 May 1948

Dear Brother: I'm in Prague for the Festival of Contemporary Music. They played my Overture today. It was a great success. I'm playing for the Radio tomorrow ... I'm taking the opportunity of being abroad to beg you, dearest little Vitek, to stop writing all those foolish things in your letters or we'll end up in jail ... All your letters are being censored in Poznań. They're being opened on the pretext of being badly sealed ...[96]

As discussed previously, the implementation of socialist realism in Polish music was debated at the 1949 conference at Łagów, which emphasised contemporary music, mass appeal, and the inclusion of folk music. Bacewicz used folk music for thematic material quite naturally; while she was comfortable with this (for her) entirely genuine form of expression, in that politically correct atmosphere, she was occasionally accused of 'formalism'. Nevertheless, 1948 was a productive year, and compositions included two of what are now her most famous pieces: *Violin Concerto No. 3* and the *Concerto for String Orchestra*.

The impact of the successful *Violin Concerto No. 3* was recognised when it received the Award of the Ministry of Culture and Fine Arts in 1955.[97] She based it on Podhale folklore, 'from which I tried to extract typical melodic phrases, harmonic juxtapositions and rhythmic features'.[98] The lyricism of the Andante was identified by Bacewicz as being based on 'a very little known but very beautiful song'[99] – using a tune from the Tatra mountains. The final Vivo is a carefree Rondo based on a swaggering oberek, a well-known folk tune from the Zakopane region.[100] Szymanowski had used this dance for the finale of his *Symphonie Concertante* for piano and orchestra. Indeed, since Bacewicz had performed Szymanowski's *Violin Concerto No. 1* in Paris, her *Concerto* also showed his influence in harmony and scoring. Its combination of lyrical warmth and great vivacity brought it immediate popularity. She played the solo part at

---

[95] See 'Symphony No. 1, Witold Lutoslawski', *Culture.pl*: https://culture.pl/en/work/symphony-no-1-witold-lutoslawski.

[96] Bacewicz (18 May 1948) in 'Letters of Grażyna Bacewicz and Vytautas Bacivicius', pp. 5–6.

[97] The 1955 Ministry of Culture and Art Award was for *Symphony No. 4* (1953), *Violin Concerto No. 3* (1948), and *String Quartet No. 3* (1947). See *String Quartet No. 3*, p. 28, and *Symphony No. 4*, p. 45.

[98] Gąsiorowska, *Bacewicz*, p. 199.

[99] Adrian Thomas, note on *Violin Concerto No. 3* in the CD booklet accompanying '*Grażyna Bacewicz Violin Concertos Nos 1, 3 and 7*' (Chandos Records Ltd., CHAN 10533, 2009), p. 6.

[100] About 250 miles south of Warsaw, in the south part of the Podhale region.

the premiere in March 1949 with the Baltic Philharmonic, and throughout the Eastern Bloc during the next few years.

Her *Concerto for String Orchestra* (1948) received the State Award, 3rd Class in 1950 and is credited as one of the most significant contributions to the genre. It was given its first public performance by the Polish Radio Symphony Orchestra and Grzegorz Fitelberg on 18 June 1950 at the General Meeting of the Polish Composers' Union.[101] Also played at the 1949 Congress of the Polish Composers' Union, it has become her most popular and most performed work and has been recorded over a dozen times. Composer and critic Stefan Kisielewski (1911–91) wrote the following review of the performance:

> The Concerto for String Orchestra, written with panache and energy, full of smooth invention and brilliant instrumentation ideas, finally stirred us from our lethargy. The piece draws on some Bach or Handel – a modern 'Brandenburg Concerto' as it were. We finally got a 'red-blooded piece' of wholesome and delicious music, written with a creative power that is truly virile.[102]

The first movement opens with a striding theme of baroque character, with motoric figurations anchored around D. The beautiful, eloquent, and richly scored Andante has a serenely flowing melody. The final Vivo is typically vivacious, combining spontaneity and acerbic harmonies. Deservedly well-liked, the music is a powerful demonstration of Bacewicz's excellence in writing for strings. Its physical vigour and strong communication make it a regular repertoire piece with chamber orchestras; buoyancy and optimism express a renewed confidence, as she and Poland recovered from World War II. In 1996, the Ambache Chamber Orchestra gave its first performance in Britain, on London's South Bank: the players relished her skilful string writing. The (London) *Times* newspaper commented on her 'cunning 13-part textures, and neo-classical energy'.[103] The vigour of her music, combined with her under-standing of string technique, gave a directness of expression which both the musicians and the audience enjoyed. The *Independent* appreciated the lively finale and described Bacewicz as 'a real expert in writing for strings'.[104]

The *Violin Sonata No. 3* (1948) was dedicated to Tadeusz Ochlewski (1894–1975), the Director of the Polish publishing house PWM, and was first performed by Bacewicz and Kiejstut in Łódź. While being imbued with folklore, it is also neo-romantic, has ironic humour, and ranges from improvisational ideas to brightly coloured musical pictures. It begins enigmatically, with an inconclusive

---

[101] See 'Concerto for String Orchestra – Grazyna Bacewicz', *Culture.pl*: https://culture.pl/en/work/concerto-for-string-orchestra-grazyna-bacewicz.

[102] S. Kisielewski (9 July 1950), cited in 'Bacewicz, Concerto for String Orchestra', *Polmic.pl*: https://bacewicz.polmic.pl/en/concerto-for-string-orchestra.

[103] The *Times*, 20 June 1996.   [104] The *Independent*, 21 June 1996.

scale creating the sense of a question – as if asking *where?* (where is the music going? – and, where are we going?). This is answered vigorously, with her usual affirmative strength. The Adagio is searching and soulful. Metrical teasing characterises the virtuosic scherzo, a march-like Vivo. A descending chromatic scale links the finale back to the opening, and this Andante includes ideas from the first movement, making an unconventional yet satisfying conclusion.

Another work completed in 1948 was her *Easy Pieces* for clarinet and piano, which show her familiar balance of imagination and emotion, while encouraging young musicians to embrace contemporary music. First, there is a pert mazurka-style Vivo. The pensive Andante has a tinge of melancholy. Next is an Allegro non troppo, with an athletic piano part involving hand-crossing, wide leaps, and fast scales; more big leaps feature in the piano part of the final Vivo. She also wrote a *Trio for Oboe, Clarinet and Bassoon* in this year. She was not very pleased with the *Trio*, but her husband stopped her from tearing up the manuscript, suggesting she could re-compose the first part; she never did. Her next work was for choir and orchestra: the short *Olympic Cantata* was based on a seventeenth-century comedy by Polish soldier and writer Piotr Baryka. It was performed by the Czech Philharmonic Orchestra at the 1948 Prague Festival. Even though it accepted socialist realism, the piece was not published. Nevertheless, in that slightly topsy-turvy world, it won the Polish State Prize and an honourable mention at the International Olympic Arts Competition London in 1948.[105]

Figure 10 Turski and Bacewicz at the Olympics, 1949

---

[105] See 'Grażyna Bacewicz: Biography', Polish Music Center.

Continuing *Chefs d'Oeuvres* (1949–50)

In 1949, Bacewicz received the Warsaw Prize for her humanitarian and creative work, given for taking an active part in the work of several charitable organisations during the War. It was a highly fertile and successful year. Her *Piano Concerto* won Second Prize (no First Prize was given) at the Polish Composers' Union Fryderyk Chopin Composition Competition in Warsaw. Medallist Stanisław Szpinalski (1901–57) gave its first performance in Warsaw and then played it round Central Europe. Piano compositions such as this one were informed by the fact that Bacewicz herself was a highly capable pianist.

The powerful unison start of the *Piano Concerto* is answered by dramatic piano arpeggios; shared dialogue follows. Stirring, muscular statements are vividly orchestrated, and folk elements colour the virtuoso solo part. The slow movement is luscious and highly atmospheric; improvisatory elements give the impression of her telling a story. The finale is a robust oberek and includes some exotic percussion. As in much of her music, this work completely belies the attitude that women only wrote pretty little pieces, and it demonstrates the truth of Kisielewski's words about her 'virile' potency (see p. 38). Actually, she loathed gender clichés, and wasn't interested in them anyway.

Other pieces composed in 1949 included her *Quartet for Four Violins*, a teaching piece probably originally written for her pupils at the Łódź Conservatory: this piece was included in the curriculum of several educational establishments.[106] In 2017, Kate Molleson, reviewing the Ambache CD of Bacewicz Chamber Music for the *Guardian*, wrote: 'try the 1949 Quartet for Four Violins as proof, with its fearless dashes from bruising dance to sparse elegy and back again. The piece is tactile and gritty; it was meant for teaching but never in a dry way.'[107] Well-written for the instruments, it demonstrates her involvement with order and formal beauty. Bacewicz's March 1947 letter from Paris (quoted previously in this Element) stated her strong feelings on the importance of shape and well-constructed music. The Allegro ma non troppo opens delicately and develops into a swaying dance; a tender Andante is followed by an energetic *Vivo* finale.

---

[106] The *Quartet for Four Violins* is included on 'Grazyna Bacewicz Chamber Music', (Ambache Recordings AMB2607, 2017): http://womenofnote.co.uk.

[107] Kate Molleson, 'CD Review: Bacewicz chamber music', the *Guardian* (2 March 2017): http://katemolleson.com/cd-review-grazyna-bacewicz-chamber-music.

In the same year, she also wrote the popular *Violin Sonata No. 4*, in which the Finale adroitly spans nineteenth-century bravura and light-hearted whimsy. Instrumental virtuosity in her music was always an integral part of the bigger, expressive picture and is most audible in her violin writing. This work is dedicated to Kiejstut. Together they gave the first performance in Warsaw, and in the mid-1950s they recorded it for the Polish Recording Company, Polskie Nagrania Muza. The sonata made impressive progress around the world, being played in the USA, London, Geneva, Prague, and Berlin. A reviewer for the *Christian Science Monitor* attended the Boston performance in February 1953:

> The Sonata No. 4 by Grażyna Bacewicz was performed in the United States for the first time. This piece was the most impressively touching and controversial of the whole program. The composer is a master of melody, which challenges the listener in the way it is expressed.[108]

The bucolic main theme of the opening Moderato of the sonata is contrasted with more tender ideas. Spread piano chords in the dark, declamatory Andante ma non troppo introduce a questioning air; the violin replies with a poignant, sombre melody; they reach accord by the end. Humorous play and vigorous interactions characterise the Molto Vivo scherzo; the Con Passione finale is more intense emotionally, mixing virtuosity with playful and dancing episodes. Among the several recordings of Bacewicz's sonatas for violin and piano are a complete set by the Akademia Muzyczna im Grażyna i Kiejstuta Becewiczów y Łodzi.[109]

Łódź people were always proud of her achievements, and the Łódź Philharmonic Orchestra organised a concert for Bacewicz on 19 February 1950 at the Philharmonic Hall.[110] The programme comprised her *Overture* (1944), *Violin Concerto No. 3* (1948), and *Piano Concerto* (1949). In July 1949, she went on a concert tour in the USSR, and Romanian conductor/ composer Constantin Silvestri (1913–69) invited her to play her *Violin Concerto No. 3* in concerts around Romania in 1950.[111] Her nine recitals there were followed by performances in Czechoslovakia, and she went on to perform with the Budapest Symphony Orchestra.

---

[108] Jules Wolffers, *Christian Science Monitor* (16 February 1953), as cited in Rosen, *Grażyna Bacewicz*.

[109] See the CD 'Grazyna Bacewicz: Sonatas for Violin and Piano', Thomasz Król (violin) and Paweł Skowroński (piano), Łódź, 2014.

[110] Archive in Akademia Muzyczna Bacewiczów, Lodz: www.amuz.lodz.pl/en.

[111] For further information, see John Gritten, *A Musician Before His Time: Constantin Silvestri – Conductor, Composer, Pianist* (London: Kitzinger, 1998).

Productivity: 1951–3

Bacewicz had many other commitments during 1950, and so there were fewer compositions. She made up for it the next year, when she again produced classical works. Returning to Warsaw, she wrote the *Cello Concerto No. 1* (1951) – probably commissioned by the MKiS as previously mentioned. The first performance was given by the Czech cellist Miloš Sádlo (1912–2003) during the Festival of Polish Music in Warsaw. In three movements, the concerto begins in a cheerful mood and includes colourful use of winds, brass, and percussion. Being both pensive and elegiac, the second movement opens with interplay between soloist and orchestra, later balanced by well-placed silences. The buoyant rhythms of the finale are countered by some teasing fun with hemiola rhythms, alternating duple and triple metre.

The breadth of her musical style in this period can be seen by contrasting the baroque figuration of the *Cello Concerto No. 1* (1951) with the grandiose *Symphony No. 4* (1953). Sometimes conservative in idiom, her larger orchestral works might have been connected to the stated public demand for impressive symphonic music. Astutely perceiving the permissible limits, she avoided censure; it is possible that the restrictions and requirements of the socialist period somehow provoked her to greater inventiveness. In her letters, she quotes Bach as a fine example of creativity within technical discipline. In a letter to her brother (23 October 1958), she wrote: 'aren't Bach's fugues beautiful despite the constraining form?'.[112]

Her massive *Symphony No. 3* was also written in 1951, but was premiered in Kraków later in September 1952; many consider it her outstanding work in the genre.[113] In a letter to Vytautus of 14 November 1966, she wrote:

> Music has changed so much in the last twenty, let alone forty years, that not only am I worried when they play my symphonies (luckily this happens very seldom) – I would never agree to a new print edition. It goes without saying that I've thrown away lots of pieces and that I would have never allowed their publication or performance.[114]

This *Third Symphony* displays remarkable integration; she created a unified structure by limiting the material, balancing monothematicism with melodic variety. The weighty opening tutti furnishes motivic ideas used in the third and fourth movements. Bacewicz's lyrical skill is also notable; here, a doleful

---

[112] Bacewicz (23 October 1958) in 'Letters of Grażyna Bacewicz and Vytautas Bacivicius', p. 9.

[113] For further details, see 'Bacewicz, *Symphony No. 3*', *Polmic.pl*: https://bacewicz.polmic.pl/en/symphony-no-3.

[114] Bacewicz (14 November 1966) in 'Letters of Grażyna Bacewicz and Vytautas Bacivičius', p. 13.

Andante contrasts broad quavers and crotchets in the outer parts with an agitated dotted rhythm in the middle section. The scherzo is a kind of orchestral fireworks display, with a trio coloured by the full brass section. Dark clouds loom at the ominous start of the Moderato finale, and the ideas are often angular and punchy. Developing into an Allegro con passione, the recapitulation leads to a Presto, and four sturdy tutti chords close the work.

As well as the symphony, this fruitful year also produced the *Violin Concerto No. 4*, the *Taniec Mazoviecki* (Mazovian Dance),[115] and the *Oberek No. 2*. The latter two bold, dance-inspired short pieces are colourful and highly evocative, showing her characteristic vitality. Unusually, the *Violin Concerto No. 4* carries a dedication – actually two: different names are given on the autograph manuscript (Kazimierz Sikorski) and on the published edition (Józef Jarzębski).[116] Both individuals were her tutors at the Warsaw Conservatoire.

The 1951 *Violin Sonata No. 5* was first performed in Kraków with Kiejstut.[117] The sonata starts with a lyrical introduction and includes hints of impressionism. The Nokturn is marked Andante dolcissimo (her music often includes an uncommon sweetness); this is almost storytelling, at times fairy tale, at others weird and eerie. The final Allegro inquietamente combines strength and more mystery, occasionally resembling a forward march. The five violin and piano sonatas (1945–51) are now part of mainstream European music. They show her thorough understanding of both instruments, adding much to the musical canon and her reputation.

The *Piano Quintet No. 1* followed in 1952. Kiejstut and the Kraków Quartet created its success in Warsaw, and it now stands among the major pieces of twentieth-century Polish chamber music.[118] The Moderato molto espressivo has a brief meditative introduction leading to an Allegro of elegant vitality; dignified playfulness is balanced with airy textures. The Presto is a typical scherzo which plays with Polish folk music, around the rhythm of an oberek. It has a poetic, somewhat mysterious middle section; a bold four-and-a-half octave glissando on the piano's white keys introduces the dynamic coda. Solemn piano chords in the style of a chorale open the stately Grave; with

---

[115] Violinist David Juritz and I recorded this dance, together with her *Polish* and *Slavonic Dances*, on the 'Bacewicz: Chamber Music' CD, AMB2607: www.womenofnote.co.uk.

[116] Bacewicz, *Violin Concerto No. 4*, PWM Edition (published edition): https://pwm.com.pl/en/wypozyczenia/utwory-wg-kategorii/publikacja/violin-concerto-no-4,bacewicz-grazyna,14887,hirelibrary.htm.

[117] See 'Bacewicz: *Sonata No. 5*', *Polmic.pl*: https://bacewicz.polmic.pl/en/sonata-no-5-for-violin-and-piano.

[118] For an in-depth view, see Terree Lee Shofner, 'The Two Piano Quintets of Grazyna Bacewicz: An Analysis of Style and Content', doctoral dissertation (Madison: University of Wisconsin, 1996), p. 11.

a heavy tread and mesmeric rhythm, the emotion ranges from mournful to defiant, developing through a cantabile melody and simple polyphony in the strings. The final Con passione is restless and dramatic, mixing reflection and action to the end. This Quintet was recorded in 1969 by the Polish pianist Władsław Szpilman (1911–2000).[119] He was evidently a good friend, as Bacewicz dedicated her *Piano Sonata No. 2* (composed in 1953) to him: 'to dear Władsław Szpilman, the excellent first interpreter of the sonata, to express true friendship, Grażyna Bacewicz, Warsaw, 15/10/1955'.[120]

Figure 11 Władysław Szpilman

As will be apparent, Bacewicz loved obereks – the dancing energy suited her temperament. As well as the two encore pieces of 1949 and 1952, they occur in the finale of the *Second Piano Sonata* and the scherzo of the 1952 *Piano Quintet*. They could have been both a safety valve in the imposed cultural atmosphere, and written from affection. YouTube has her 1952 performance of one of her *Obereks,* with Kiejstut at the piano; with her sturdy technique as a violinist, her playing has poise and focus.[121] Apparently, she composed the first *Oberek* as an encore for an impending concert; indeed, many other of her shorter pieces are sometimes now used as curtain-calls.

---

[119] Szpilman became internationally famous following Roman Polanski's film *The Pianist* (2002), which was inspired by Szpilman's wartime memoirs. See Małgorzata Kosińska, 'Władsław Szpilman', *Culture.pl*: https://culture.pl/en/artist/wladyslaw-szpilman.

[120] An image of Bacewicz's written inscription to Szpilman on the score of her sonata can be found at 'From Sony Classical Germany: Władsław Szpilman Legendary Recordings' on Władsław Szpilman's website: www.szpilman.net/framemain.html.

[121] 'Bacewicz plays Bacewicz – *Oberek* (1952)': www.youtube.com/watch?v=Y4H-GapUP78.

Violin Concerto No. 4 and *String Quartet No. 4*

The *Violin Concerto No. 4* was written at the height of the Stalinist regime and was premiered in Kraków, early in 1952.[122] Again, Bacewicz doesn't seem to have been limited by the cultural policy of the day. The concerto shows increased harmonic colour, creating tension from adjacent tones and semitones. There is high energy, and a somewhat rustic, Slavic feel; the first movement is darker than in her previous concertos. This is a virtuoso work, including varied articulation, exceedingly fast tempi, and frequent use of double-stopping, stylised in a folk-like manner. In 1952, Bacewicz was awarded the Polish National Prize, and this concerto was cited as one of three contributing works (with her *String Quartet No. 4* and her *Violin Sonata No. 4*).

As the Polish socialist government followed the Soviet line of art for the masses, repressing creativity, composers balanced their personal, imaginative instincts with public requirements. Managing such pressures, Bacewicz was the foremost exponent of non-programmatic music and, as an individual, she kept the genre of the string quartet alive during the post-war decade.[123] The ZKP (the Union) commissioned her work for submission to the String Quartet Competition in Liège. The Quatuor Municipal de Liège premièred her *String Quartet No. 4* in September 1951, and it won First Prize at the First International Competition for Composers of a String Quartet.[124] A Belgian critic wrote in *Le Monde du travail*:

> The language of the 'Quartet' is more classical than those of the other Quartets performed during the same audition. Its melody is fuller and, one could say, more tradition-oriented. The elegiac introduction is followed by fantastic themes that soon mingle with other musical thoughts, and breathing becomes faster. The slow movement attains a level which one cannot notice in other quartets. This quiet meditation and logically constructed fugato reveal extraordinary mental qualities and a truly musical temper. Again, it is Beethoven that comes to mind, this time from his last Quartets, especially in Rondo, where a Polish folk dance intertwines with episodes of a reflexive nature.[125]

Bacewicz had been reluctant to send her work into the Liège Competition, but her brother Kiejstut and the eminent Polish violinist Irena Dubiska persuaded her to do so. It won, out of fifty-seven entries. The success continued: the *Fourth*

---

[122] See 'Bacewicz, *Violin Concerto No. 4*', *Polmic.pl*: https://bacewicz.polmic.pl/en/concerto-no -4-for-violin-and-orchestra.

[123] I am in agreement with Adrian Thomas on this point. See Thomas, 'Review of Bacewicz Chamber Works', *Notes, Second Series*, vol. 60/2 (December 2003): 546.

[124] 'Bacewicz, *String Quartet No. 4*', *Polmic.pl*: https://bacewicz.polmic.pl/en/string-quartet-no-4.

[125] Marcel Lemaire, *Le Monde du Travail* (3 October 1951), cited in 'Bacewicz, *String Quartet No. 4*', *Culture.pl* : https://culture.pl/en/work/string-quartet-no-4-grazyna-bacewicz.

Quartet was awarded the National Prize in 1952, and it was chosen as the set piece for the 1953 International Chamber Music Competition at Geneva, growing in fame.

String Quartet No. 4 starts with an elegiac introduction; the first movement then alternates between Andante and Allegro energico sections. A rather simple folksong is later contrasted with harsh, dissonant passages. Lyrical and contemplative, the slow movement is serene – meditative themes lead to a fugato. The third movement dominates the work by grafting older dance forms with baroque reminiscences. Folk music is fundamental to the piece; the jaunty Allegro giocoso is a lively oberek, with repetitions and variations; like an instrumental ricercar, it alternates toccata-style passages with the contrapuntal treatment of the main theme.

The year 1951 ended with a December concert in Liège (which included Bacewicz's own works): a duo recital in which she performed with the pianist Monique Pichon. Then she became a frequent guest as soloist in Belgium, with Pichon. In a series entitled Concerts Gretry,[126] she performed music by Tartini, Leclair, Mozart, Wieniawski, Szymanowski, and herself.

Thoughts on Modern Music

Throughout this highly productive time, Bacewicz was ruminating on her own work as a composer. Writing to her brother in 1952, she explained her thoughts on modern music and how she was paid:

16 February 1952

Dear Vitek: The problem you've mentioned in your letter is my old problem, too . . . You see, I've realized a couple of years ago that composers have really ended up in an impasse with all that avant-garde. And something had to be done about it. To go on didn't make any sense. In fact, compositions no longer pleased even the composers themselves (remarkable geniuses excluded). Music is a beautiful art; the things written were not.

There has also been a change in my own experience and understanding of music. I decided a new road had to be found. It should lead above all through a simplification of the musical language. A simplification, not a return to the old ways of classicism, of the major-minor system – the quest for the simple and the new, obviously without denying the achievements of the previous epoch, by which I mean the entire first half of the 20th century.

Apart from that, composers seem to be ashamed of their emotional side – so I've thrown all caution to the wind and I now write emotional music. I'm not saying I've already found that new road, for that might take a whole century and dozens of composers. Still, I'm searching, I'm concentrating and, above all, I'm trying to write earnestly.

---

[126] Named after Liège composer André-Ernest-Modeste Grétry (1741–1813).

I've come to the conclusion during my stay in Belgium that Western composers are going nowhere . . . They're still fooling around with noises, colours, interesting rhythms etc., but still there's no Music there.

I have a test for my own road being not too bad, since my Quartet won first prize despite being jotted down in no time between one thing and another! Obviously, I'm as far as I could possibly be from saying I've achieved perfection! The West might be playing with their little noises, but I think they've had enough. As to myself, I keep on being tackled (despite all success) for writing 'tough' music – which seems to be the general opinion of my work. Yet as long as I'm not convinced my stuff's too complex, I'll keep on doing what I'm doing now.

I think you've been misinformed on the 'commission' system here. In fact, it's a wonderful thing that's making the whole Western Europe green with envy. We're being paid by the state so that we can work in tranquillity. Did Bach write a single piece that didn't have to be commissioned? And I'd rather get the money from the state than from an individual. You're also wrong in believing commissions are only for mass songs. I get contracts for quartets, symphonies, concertos, pedagogical pieces (I like that) etc. The commissions might display certain tendencies – for instance, to produce operas and cantatas accessible to the general public – but, in general, one does what one does best . . . .

A composer must write honestly, for inner satisfaction, yet without forgetting his audience. Gr.[127]

Her awareness of the expressive limits of avant-garde technique was echoed by others. She was sure enough of her own ideas not to be affected by what was then in fashion, and so she stuck with her own manner. Her personal integrity kept her true to her individual approach, happily likening the way she was commissioned to Bach's work for his church employers.

Works for Piano, a Symphony, and a Ballet

All four movements of her (unpublished) 1949 *Piano Sonata No. 1* are in some version of ternary form, and there is a simple unity among the themes. The work maintains a light-hearted mood, with a national colour (oberek and mazurka): the manuscript is in the National Library of Poland. Although Bacewicz was not fond of this sonata, she used some of the musical material in her orchestral works. The sonata and her *Krakowiak* of 1949 were submitted to the Chopin Competition for Composers in Warsaw and together were awarded Third Prize.

Written four years later, *Piano Sonata No. 2* (1952–3) is now deemed her most significant piano work.[128] The requirements of Stalinist repression are less in evidence here, and the piece could be said to be going against socialist realist demands; likely, she was caricaturing folk elements. This author's opinion is

---

[127] Bacewicz letter (16 February 1952) in 'Letters of Grażyna Bacewicz and Vytautas Bacivicius', pp. 6–7.
[128] See 'Bacewicz, *Piano Sonata no 2*', *Polmic.pl*: https://bacewicz.polmic.pl/en/piano-sonata-no-2.

that she was not arguing with *socrealizm*, but staying true to her own manner. The *Second Sonata*'s first movement has Lisztian virtuosity. The music starts with volcanic energy – it is vivid and highly wrought. Much of it is *appassionato*; there is great strength, with semi-quavers played at rattling speed. Then, it is tempered by some solemn Andante music, and it cranks up again to a massive end. She produces variety through symmetry, irregularity (seven changes of meter in the first eleven bars), and cross-rhythms. Bass clef chords clash with treble minor thirds, creating harmonic and melodic tension.

The simple Lento movement is designed in a palindromic form ABCDCBA. Her fondness for augmented seconds suggests a folk element, and then an eerie *poco meno* gradually expands into dramatic, vehement writing. Chromaticism gives melodic shading, and rhythmic diminution announces a new Agitato section. The dazzling last movement is slightly skittish. This finale juxtaposes the *moto perpetuo* rhythms of a neo-baroque Toccata with a vivacious oberek; it is quirky and ever more exciting. As her Warsaw training had included piano studies, Bacewicz was a highly capable player. In 1953 she also appeared as a concert pianist at a piano recital organised by the Polish Composers Union and premiered her *Piano Sonata No. 2* and then later recorded it. Krystian Zimerman recorded a dazzling CD version of it in 2011 for Deutsche Grammophon.[129]

Bacewicz wrote the *Symphony No. 4* in 1953, and it was her last orchestral work.[130] It was dedicated to Grzegorz Fitelberg and premièred in Kraków on 15 January 1954 by conductor Bohdan Wodiczko (1911–85) and the National Philharmonic. It won the Ministry of Culture and Arts Award in 1955. For large orchestra, with powerful climaxes, it seems as if Bacewicz is making light of the straitjacket imposed on composers.

In February 1953, she went back to Paris to be a member of the jury of the Margaret Long and Jacques Thibaut Competition.[131] That December she completed her first ballet, *A Peasant Transformed into a King*, based on Świniarski's libretto on Baryka's 1637 comedy.[132] It is built on a story regularly told in

---

[129] This Deutsche Grammophon recording is also available on YouTube: www.youtube.com /watch?v=8pBWVTNdHoY.

[130] 'Bacewicz, *Symphony No. 4*', *Polmic.pl*: https://bacewicz.polmic.pl/en/symphony-no-4.

[131] Bacewicz was invited to serve as a member of the jury on several international competitions at this time. In 1952, for instance, she served as a member of the jury of international violin competitions in Liège and Poznań for the Henry Wieniawski International Violin Competition. See 'Bacewicz Biography', Polish Music Center, University of Southern California and 'Bacewicz', International Wieniawski Violin Competition: www.wieniawski.com/bacewicz_ grazyna.html.

[132] Bacewicz, *A Peasant Transformed into a King*, PWM Edition: https://pwm.com.pl/en/wypo zyczenia/utwory-wg-kategorii/publikacja/a-peasant-into-a-king-transformed,bacewicz-grazyna,13404,hirelibrary.html.

European literature – about some practical jokers dressing up a drunken peasant as a king to make fun of him. The musical characterisation of the two milieus, the local peasantry and the court circles, combines stylised dances of the seventeenth and eighteenth centuries with Polish folk ideas.

Misfortune and Progress in 1954

At the height of this time of great recognition, Bacewicz was involved in a serious car accident. In the early autumn of 1954, on a Sunday family excursion to a lake near Gabin (by Sochaczew, forty miles from Warsaw), a truck ran their car into a ditch, smashing it into a steel pole. Her immediate family received minor injuries, but Bacewicz and her mother-in-law were seriously hurt; she was partly disabled, with a broken pelvis, cracked ribs, and injuries to her head and face. Village women gathered round while she was repeating, 'I broke my pelvis'.[133] The Polish word *miednic* means both pelvis and wash basin; Bacewicz imagined they thought she was raving. What helped her through her crisis was obsessively listening in her head to an F minor fugue by Bach (music that saved her at other bad times). Friends who visited her in hospital described her demeanour: 'There she was fighting for her life, and though she had difficulty talking, she spent the time joking and refusing to discuss the accident or the seriousness of her condition.'[134] Although she was a long time in hospital, she resumed composing immediately after she was out. She also continued to participate in public life, serving as Vice-Chair of the Polish Composers Union from 1955 to 1957.

The year 1954 was also a significant time for Bacewicz's younger colleague Andrzej Panufnik, who was considered at this time to be among the most successful composers working in Poland. At the forefront of Polish music-making, he had direct experience of Soviet domination of cultural policy. Tired of serving the communist state in Poland, he fled the country in 1954, citing being asked to spy during foreign orchestra visits as his reason for leaving. Lutosławski's *Concerto for Orchestra* was premiered on 26 November 1954 and brought recognition for him in the West.

In 1954, Bacewicz composed her *Polish Overture*. With a march-like forward momentum, there is strength and pride in this overture. The clarinet is prominent, and the winds and brass feature in the imaginative middle section; the earlier cheerfulness returns, with some teasing time changes. Although she was able to continue composing, she withdrew from the concert platform following her car accident. The soloist in the first performance of her *Violin Concerto*

---

[133] Bacewicz, 'Ravings' in *A Distinguishing Mark*, p. 80.
[134] Kisielewski, *Grażyna Bacewicz I jej czasy* (Kraków: PWM, 1963), p. 34.

No. 5 (also written in 1954) was Wanda Wiłkomirska (1929–2018),[135] with conductor Witold Rowicki and the Warsaw Philharmonic Orchestra. This concerto returned somewhat toward ideas of the *Violin Concerto No. 3*: there are bittersweet drones, a primitive ostinato, and triadic harmony in two keys together. In the gritty and challenging Deciso, some of the angst is alleviated by a thoughtful violin cadenza. The Andante has a magical orchestral opening, with atmospheric upper-strings tremolos over ominous lower strings. Confident in mood, the finale has folk colour and buoyant rhythms; the soloist is literally riding high, which leads to a fizzing conclusion.

Songs

Although Bacewicz is perhaps best known for her orchestral and chamber works at this time, her 'middle' period included most of her song compositions; she wrote a dozen between 1934 and 1956. The intimate form of solo voice and keyboard depends on the interpretation of a poem or text and is a particular test of a composer's insight. Bacewicz was probably linked to singing by her choirmaster father, and she understood the power of poetry and the expressivity of the human voice. From her violin playing and composing, she had a fine lyrical sense. Her keyboard skills also meant she appreciated the voice and piano partnership.

Influences might have included the Polish song-writer and Romantic composer Stanisław Moniuszko (1819–72). A nationalist, he incorporated patriotic folk themes, such as the popular krakowiaczek, in his songs. The later Romantic Mieczysław Karłowicz (1876–1909) set words by poets of the Young Poland movement. Szymanowski wrote several groups of songs, some with connections to Polish folk music, others on words by Tadeusz Miciński, Tagore, and James Joyce.

In the 1930s, Bacewicz had written *Three Songs* on tenth-century Arabic poems from *The Garden of Caresses*, orchestrating them in 1938. These songs showed her thoughtful response to poetry and its potential for word painting. The Tagore setting 'Mów do mnie, miły' ('Speak to Me, My Love') came in 1936, with a second use of his poetry in 1949 – 'Rozstanie' (an emotional response to 'Parting'). Twice she used words by the Polish poet Konstanty Ildefons Gałczyński (1905–53):[136] 'Here Is the Night' (1947) and 'Lips and Fullness' (1949). Later she set words by Adam Mickiewicz (1798–1855),[137] who was counted as one of Poland's Three Bards: the most charming was

---

[135] See 'Wanda Wilkomirska', *Culture.pl*: https://culture.pl/en/artist/wanda-wilkomirska.

[136] See 'Konstanty Ildefons Gałczyński', *Culture.pl*: https://culture.pl/en/artist/konstanty-ildefons-galczynski.

[137] See 'Adam Mickiewicz', *Culture.pl*: https://culture.pl/en/artist/adam-mickiewicz

'Dzwon i dzwonki' ('Bells and Ringing', 1955). Her last song was 'Sroczla' ('Little Magpie', 1956), based on light-hearted folk verse. PWM have published a collection of her songs, which range through storytelling, love poems, to sadness from absence – possibly forming an unintended thematic series. Kiejstut described them as follows:

> Grażyna's songs are decidedly intimate in nature, as regards both the expressive settings of the texts and the compositional principles adopted. They are fine musical poems, arranged in an ingenious and elaborate way [as] duets for voice and piano ... . An atmosphere of intense concentration prevails. Emotional content of the songs is very sublime. There is a refined play of symbols involved.[138]

Violin Music

As well as her five violin and piano sonatas, Bacewicz also wrote several short violin and piano pieces in the late 1940s and early 1950s, many reflecting her folk interests; some are played as encores. One of her most popular violin pieces, *Capriccio* from 1946, is (naturally) capricious; after a broadly thoughtful introduction, there is some rousing, show-off violin action. These are all part of her fulsome contribution to Polish twentieth-century music. There are two *Obereks, –* a fast Mazurka-style dance (1948 and 1951). This favourite, a lively Polish national dance (from *obracić się* – to spin), has acrobatic elements, with dance lifts and jumps. There are some other robust folk dances: *Polish Dance* (1948), *Mazovian Dance* (1951), and *Slavonic Dance* (1952). When I recorded these works with violinist David Juritz, we were both taken with Bacewicz's effective use of the folk styles combined with brilliant violin writing.[139] Her interest in folk music meant that she responded to the unique accents of the different areas. The *Polish Dance* is like a krakoviak, in which the steps include running, shuffling, and 'hołubiec' (clicking heels). Mazovia is located in east-central Poland; the composer had spent some of the war in a camp in Pruszków (central Poland), going on to Grodzisk Mazowiecki and Lublin. The *Slavonic Dance* features a driving, repetitive drone note under a syncopated tune.

Additionally for violin and piano, the *Cradle Song* is gently rocking. The *Antique Dance* of 1950 returns to neoclassical form, while the whimsical *Humoresque* of 1953 is mostly in 5/8 time. Affirming Bacewicz's national identity, the folk works also gave her some shelter from the new atonal and twelve-tone styles. The music is part of her interest in providing her students with

---

[138] Kiejstut Bacewicz as cited in PWM Edition *Grazyna Bacewicz: Collected Songs*: https://pwm .com.pl/en/sklep/publikacja/collected-songs,grazyna-bacewicz,2538,shop.html.

[139] On the 'Grazyna Bacewicz: Chamber Music' CD (Ambache Recordings, 2017).

stimulating music to play. She was an outstanding player whose mastery of the violin and understanding of virtuosity rooted her compositions in a deeply felt language and successful use of the instrument.

From the Ground Up

By the 1950s, Bacewicz had succeeded in establishing a commanding profile as an exceptional composer and brilliant solo violinist in state-controlled Poland. In 1957, war correspondent Martha Gellhorn (1908–98) reported on the arts in Communist Poland in *The View from the Ground*:

> In Warsaw, you also remember that you are in a Communist-controlled country, though by all accounts the control is now humane and lenient, judged by what it was and what it is in other satellite countries. Still you do hear the incompetent echo in the tapped hotel telephone; you do notice that people look over their shoulders when talking in restaurants – the secret police are dormant but not forgotten; you feel in your bones, as you would feel a threatening change in the weather, every change in Russian mood or action. This is not an air we have ever breathed; I doubt if we would be strong enough to resist such a climate and stay as healthy in spirit as the Poles.[140]

Figure 12 Palace of Culture and Science

---

[140] Gellhorn, 'Home of the Brave' in *The View from the Ground* (New York: Atlantic Monthly Press, 1988).

The tallest building in Poland was constructed from 1952 to 1955 in Warsaw and exemplified relations with the Soviet Union; the Joseph Stalin Palace of Culture and Science was a 'gift' from Stalin. It is a divisive and controversial construction; the Poles are still not happy about it and have given it various nicknames, from The Russian Wedding Cake to *Chuj Stalina* (*Stalin's Dick*). The dedication to Stalin was later removed, and now it houses an exhibition centre, office complex, cinemas, theatres, museums, and (a sign of the times) a casino.

3 Finale: 1955–69

Part 1: 1955–60

After Stalin's death in 1953, there was new artistic activity in satellite nations, and Poland started steering a more independent course. From the mid-1950s, the 'Khrushchev Thaw' was a period of relaxing of Soviet censorship and meant a partial liberalisation. Anti-communist resistance grew, notably in the industrial city of Poznań.[141] In 1956, the stirrings of political and social unrest erupted there, with strikes starting in June.[142] The local Polish workers rioted, protesting against the Russian regime of political terror and low standards of living. The result was more tolerant Polish Communist Party rule that allowed increased freedom: the International Festival of Contemporary Music was the musical expression of this.[143]

With multiple injuries from her car accident in 1954, Bacewicz had spent a long time recovering in hospital; but her brain was as active as ever. Community-minded, Bacewicz served a two-year term as Vice-President of the Polish Union of Composers from 1955. Compositionally, her horizons were still expanding; her last work for violin and piano was the 1955 *Partita*. The movements alternate slow/reflective and fast/exuberant. The Praeludium and Intermezzo express notable melancholy and come from the heart. The opening Grave is a lugubrious dirge, with a trudging, funereal piano part and a growling bass; a yearning melodic line is offset by the piano's low, semi-tonal rocking. In contrast, movements two and four are effervescent *tours de force* for both violin and piano. The Toccata (second) is an exciting *moto perpetuo*, with driving repeated notes. Only thirty-nine bars long, the unearthly musing of the Andante melancolico gives a brief respite from the

---

[141] See 'Poznań Riots', *Encyclopaedia Britannica*: www.britannica.com/event/Poznan-Riots.

[142] Social unrest was also building in Hungary in 1956, which in October turned into the Hungarian Revolution against Soviet-imposed policies.

[143] Anna Iwanicka-Nijakowski, 'Warsaw Autumn International Festival of Contemporary Music', *Culture.pl*: https://culture.pl/en/article/warsaw-autumn-international-festival-of-contemporary -music.

action; the melodic line unfolds against a chiming backdrop. The dashing Rondo includes violin techniques such as *spiccato* (bouncing the bow for a staccato effect), pizzicato chords, and double stops, generating a bubbling energy, spiced with irregular accents. A playful sense of motor movement gives great impetus to this finale, which has an impulsive end. She wrote two versions of the *Partita,* one with piano and the other with orchestra; it became a kind of iconic work of hers.

On Tour and the Warsaw Autumn Festival

Representing Polish composers, Bacewicz went on a tour of India in 1956 with sculptor Tadeusz Kulisiewicz (1899–1988), writer Wilhelm Mach (1917–65), and lawyer Szymon Gottesman (1886–1955). This engaging interaction with Indian culture appears in her short stories, which describe discovering the contrasting cultures of Poles and Indians: not knowing that Indian music would last from 6 pm to 6 am, Bacewicz was puzzled by their very long performances. Because Indian music is improvised, the Indians had difficulty understanding Bacewicz as a performer, separate from being a composer.[144] After visiting some famous elephants carved from a single block of stone, the Poles gave a concert to people who hadn't encountered Western music before. The singer held a long high note, and the children burst out laughing – by joining in the laughter they remained good friends. Besides performing in this rural concert, Bacewicz also played in Delhi, Bombay, and Calcutta.

On her way home, Bacewicz and her companions visited Egypt and went to see an oasis; she became engaged in watching the beautiful movement of the dunes created by the wind. Their Arab chauffeur suddenly set off at great speed, and when they said they didn't want to die from his hurry, the driver explained that nor did he – there was a hurricane coming.[145] The year 1956 included more travel for Bacewicz, to Italy and Belgium as well as Egypt and India; and in the following year, she went to Geneva for the International Conference of the Music Festivals.[146]

Bacewicz was also involved in establishing the Warsaw Autumn Festival at this time. In June 1955, the Polish Composers Union (ZKP) initiated talks with the state authorities to organise regular festivals of contemporary

---

[144] Bacewicz, 'Are you afraid of the Stranger?', *A Distinguishing Mark*, p. 37.

[145] Bacewicz, 'Please Stop', in ibid., p. 42.

[146] She was joined at the 1957 Conference by the distinguished Polish pianist Zbigniew Drzewiecki (1890–1971), who had assisted in establishing the International Chopin Piano Competition in 1927. For the history of the Chopin Piano Competition, see 'Międzynarodowsky Konkurs Pianistyczny im. Fryderyka Chopina', *Fryderyk Chopin Institute*: https://en.chopin.nifc.pl/insti tute/chopincompetition/info.

music.[147] Bacewicz was part of the organising committee, and in a radio interview of 2 October 1956 she said:

> There is huge interest in our Warsaw Festival and many people asked me for an invitation. But I wasn't authorized to invite them, because the list of our guests had already been closed. ... On my way to Belgium I visited Paris. I spent some three weeks there with my daughter. I was there on official business. I had to get in touch with the *Orchestre National de la Radiodiffusion*, which will come to our contemporary music festival .... I visited some people, including my beloved professor Nadia Boulanger.[148]

The new musical celebration, the Warsaw Autumn, included works by leading avant-garde composers (e.g. Stockhausen and Schaeffer); younger Polish composers also came forward, including Krzysztof Penderecki (1933–2020), Henryk Górecki (1933–2010), and Kazimierz Serocki (1922–81). Reportedly, the Festival played a significant role in the establishment of a 'Polish composers' school,[149] which featured the importance of tone colour. This substantial international event signaled that *socrealizm* was coming to an end; with a sense of relief, creative people in Poland started abandoning it around 1953.

The first Warsaw Autumn took place in October 1956.[150] It aimed to present new Polish and international music, and was indeed cosmopolitan: music by Stravinsky, Schoenberg, Berg, Bartók, Shostakovich, Honegger, and Prokofiev was performed. Bacewicz was one of six Polish composers featured, and her *String Quartet No. 4, Concerto for String Orchestra*, and the *Overture* were included: her music has been part of the Festival since then. The 69-year-old Nadia Boulanger (1887–1979) attended this 1956 event as guest of honour; the Festival also played music by former Boulanger students, including Zygmunt Mycielski (1907–87, editor of the music magazine *Ruch Muzyczny*) and Kazimierz Serocki (past Vice-President of the Polish National Composers' Union and one of the organisers of the Festival).

The Festival ended the isolation from Western musical trends, and Poles heard works by Webern, Messiaen, Schoenberg, and Berg for the first time. Encountering modern ideas was most valuable for the younger generation of composers, but subtle changes also occurred in Bacewicz's style: ever true to herself, she evolved gradually, in her own way. As Judith Rosen has noted, three paths of development show in her music from this time: (1) movement away from tonality; (2) greater focus on instrumental colour; and (3) further development of rhythmical

---

[147] See 'Bacewicz – In the Shadow of the Warsaw Autumn', *Polmic.pl*: https://bacewicz.polmic.pl /en/in-the-shadow-of-the-warsaw-autumn.

[148] Bacewicz, cited in ibid.

[149] See '1960s Polish School of Composition' on Map of Polish Composers Timeline, Adam Mickiewicz Institute, *Polska Music*: https://mapofcomposers.pl/en.

[150] See 'Warsaw Autumn International Festival of Contemporary Music', *Culture.pl*; https:// culture.pl/en/article/warsaw-autumn-international-festival-of-contemporary-music.

Figure 13 Grażyna Bacewicz, Nadia Boulanger, Kazimierz Serocki, 1956

patterns.[151] These can be seen in the *String Quartet No. 5* (1955), the *Violin Concerto No. 6* (1957), and particularly in the *Symphonic Variations* (1957). Expressing relief from *socrealizm* ending – six months after the first Festival – Lutosławski spoke at the 9th General Assembly of the Polish Composers' Union on 9 March 1957:

> Our Assembly, for the first time in a long while, takes place in an atmosphere of true creative freedom. No one here will persecute anybody for so-called formalism, no one will try to prevent anybody else from expressing his aesthetic opinions, regardless of what individual composers represent. When today, from the perspective of eight and a half years, I look back on the notorious conference in Łagow in 1949 … I go cold just remembering that dreadful experience. In fact, it is hard [to find] a more absurd argument than this – that one should erase the output of recent decades and return to the musical language of the nineteenth century … The period of which I speak may not have lasted long, because it actually passed a couple of years ago, but it was nevertheless long enough to have visited tremendous damage on our music. The psyche of a creative artist is an extremely delicate and precise instrument. So the attack on that instrument and the attempt to subdue it caused not a few of us moments of severe depression.[152]

---

[151] Rosen, *Grażyna Bacewicz*.

[152] Lutosławski, cited in Adrian Thomas, 'Lutosławski Speaks Out (1957)', *On Polish Music*: https://onpolishmusic.com/2013/03/09/•-wl10023-9-10-march-1957.

New Directions

Encountering electronic music and the works of Stockhausen and Boulez at Warsaw Autumn Festivals opened up new creative avenues for Polish composers. Bacewicz recognised these new directions; in a 1958 letter to her friend, composer Witold Rudziński (1913–2004), she wrote:

> I needed to find another path in my writing. We need to simplify the language of music, finding something new without negating work of the past. I am certain of an argument for the dodecaphonic writers. I am always creating and this serial system interests me but doesn't give the entire answer. The greater part of today's composers work systematically to put ideas in order. If there is no connecting vein this takes away from the field of activity. Even though dodecaphonic music does not tell me everything, I work out my own system.[153]

Fresh ideas can be found in her *String Quartet No. 5* (1955) – including new instrumental colour combinations, further experiments with rhythm, motivic development, and an abandonment of tonality.[154] This highly expressive *String Quartet* went beyond folk-music-making and has adventurous, non-diatonic harmonic language. With a Beethovenian intensity and rare integration, this is the most individual of Bacewicz's *Quartets*. No longer drawing on folk music, it represents expressive and technical advances on its predecessor. The first movement achieves an uncommon dramatic balance between the kinetic energy of the first subject group and the remote stillness of the second. The Scherzo is a double fugue of great wit and verve. The Largo 'Corale' is one of the most notable of Bacewicz's slow movements – quiet solemnity contrasts with animated short fugatos. The final variations go from a grotesque dance, via a satirical dotted rhythm and Giocoso, mock-Vivaldi passage work, to a good-natured Vivace coda. Writing to her brother about this *Fifth String Quartet*, she recorded her thoughts about the twelve-tone technique and staying on her own path:

19 October 1957

Dear Vitek: You once wrote about musical creation in a way that made me think it might be a good idea for you to contact dodecaphonists. As you probably know, there is a fairly large group of composers in France, West Germany and Italy who venture upon untrodden ways. You might be interested, I think. They're all derived from dodecaphony, but they're on a road of their own. The whole thing is based on the concept of

---

153 Cited in Gąsiorowska, *Bacewicz*, p. 158. See also 'Witold Rudziński', Polish Music Center: https://polishmusic.usc.edu/research/composers/witold-rudzinski.

154 On her way back from India, she learnt that this piece had won Second Prize in the 1956 Liège International Competition of Chamber Music. She took her daughter, Alina, to Holland, Belgium, and Paris, staying for over a month, in order to acquaint her with Flemish paintings and to see the Louvre Museum.

series. It's a totally new formal problem that's of the greatest interest, and it's also new in terms of tone (instrumentation). It's mostly Boulez in France, Stockhausen in Germany, and Luigi Nono in Italy. They're all pretty well known in Europe. I'll stick to my 'conservatism' (the inverted commas are included because my music is perceived as 'wild' here), although of course I'm trying to keep abreast of what's going on in the world at large. I shall not follow those gentlemen because it wouldn't be honest on my part and I find honesty the most important thing in art. My music is emotional, perhaps somewhat in the old sense; their music creates emotion with completely different qualities: the perfection of conducting the series etc, etc, and that's what makes me recoil from it . . .

Love from us all – Grażyna[155]

Bacewicz chose not to publish her *Violin Concerto No. 6* (1957): Wanda said that 'Grażyna deleted it – since the music is used in her other works'.[156] Half an hour long, with substantial scoring (full brass, harp, and percussion), the concerto includes a beautiful slow movement, and the finale has a great sense of fun.[157] Also composed in 1957, the (published) *Symphonic Variations* were premiered by Jan Krenz and the Polish Radio Orchestra at the 1958 Warsaw Autumn Festival.[158] Bacewicz wrote fewer pieces for full orchestra in the second half of the 1950s, and the *Variations* was her last work of this time displaying a strong connection with folk music. A fresh approach to orchestral writing can be detected in the piece – each group is treated with equal importance; and she also produced new qualities through varying registers, quicker changes in texture, and independent handling of individual instruments (especially percussion). Parading instrumental colour with considerable orchestral virtuosity, the *Symphonic Variations* demonstrate how smoothly Bacewicz began to adopt the elements of new techniques while staying with her own musical world.

Popular with pianists, and a personal favourite of Bacewicz herself, the *Ten Études* (1956) were played at the second Warsaw Autumn (1957) by virtuoso Regina Smendzianka (1924–2011).[159] Smendzianka said of the piece:

Her *Études* are masterly and free from any folkloristic reminiscences, yet they are full of technical difficulties, providing a fine incentive even to

---

[155] Bacewicz (19 October 1957) in 'Letters of Grażyna Bacewicz and Vytautas Bacivičius', p. 8.

[156] Wanda Bacewicz in *Grażyna Bacewicz* (film), 1999. This action perhaps relates to Bacewicz's increased recycling of ideas in her later music.

[157] Although the score of this Concerto remains unpublished, there is now a YouTube recording by Bartłomiej Nizioł and the Filharmonia Narodowa. See 'Bacewicz – *Violin Concerto No. 6*', performed on 7 December 2019 by Bartłomiej Nizioł (violin), Christoph Konig (conductor), Filharmonia Narodowa / Warsaw Philharmonic Orchestra: www.youtube.com/watch?v=ZTJ7rWwPnEY.

[158] See 'Bacewicz, *Symphonic Variations*', *Polmic.pl*: https://bacewicz.polmic.pl/en/variations-for-orchestra.

[159] A performance by Regina Smendzianka of Bacewicz's *10 Etudes/Studies for Piano* is available on YouTube: www.youtube.com/watch?v=BICi2w-wfEY.

concert pianists. They indicate that Bacewicz, a pianist herself, must have been very accomplished.[160]

Bacewicz was also combining composition with public work at this time. Dedicated to her fellow artists, she participated as juror in important violin competitions. In 1957, she chaired the jury (which included David Oistrakh and Frederick Grinke) of the third Wieniawski International Violin Competition, and in 1958 served on the panel of the first Tchaikovsky Competition in Moscow.[161]

Violin, Radio, and *Music for Strings, Trumpets and Percussion*

Bacewicz's *Sonata for Violin Solo No. 2* was written in 1958.[162] It explores the wide range of technical and expressive possibilities of the violin and is a bold, modernist piece; it has a long slow movement, sandwiching two short, quick ones. There is considerable thematic and metrical freedom, some furious displays of bowing in the finale, and it ends audaciously with three big pizzicati. In November of that same year, Polish Radio commissioned Bacewicz to write a comic opera based on an old Celtic legend. They broadcast the first performance, and it was aired later on Belgian Radio and Polish Television. She wrote *The Adventure of King Arthur* to a libretto by Edward Fiszer.[163] In this work, a riddle is set by a giant to a king – 'What do all women desire?':

> While King Arthur is banqueting with his Knights, a frightened Maiden bursts in and tells of the Giant, a great lover of virgins, ravaging the surrounding countryside. Arthur sets off to conquer him, but being defeated, he has to agree to the Giant's conditions: within three days he must solve a brain-teaser about what women want, or be killed. In the castle, King Arthur has assembled worldly-wise matrons, innocent maidens, charming ladies, slaves and milk-maids to ask their advice. He

---

[160] Smendzianka, quoted in B. M. Maciejewski, *Twelve Polish Composers* (London: Allegro Press, 1976), pp. 73–4.

[161] 'The International Tchaikovsky Competition': https://tchaikovskycompetition.com/en/about.

[162] This piece is included on Chandos Records' 'Bacewicz: Works for Violin and Piano' (Chan 10250), performed by Joanna Kurkowicz (violin) and Gloria Chien (pian0). See Jonathan Woolf's review of this CD on the *Music Web International* website: www.musicweb-international.com/classrev/2004/Nov04/Bacewicz.html.

[163] Grażyna Bacewicz, *Przygoda Krola Artura / The Adventures of King Arthur*, performance by Polish Radio, 2009. Details available at *Feel the Blues with All That Jazz*: http://theblues-thatjazz.com/en/classical/595-gfrazynabacewicz/24039-grayna-bacewicz–przygoda-krola-artura-the-adventure-of-king-arthur-2009.html. See also Bacewicz, *The Adventures of King Arthur, Polmic.pl*: https://bacewicz.polmic.pl/en/the-adventure-of-king-arthur-radio-opera.

receives different answers: love, jewellery, children's happiness, a husband, health. These are then presented to the Giant by King Arthur; but all are wrong. The Giant gives the King one more chance: the deadline for solving the riddle is extended. An old Witch promises to help Arthur in exchange for a young husband. The King agrees to marry the horrible Witch, who during the wedding night is transformed into a beautiful girl (under a spell, she lives as an old woman for twelve hours and as a young beauty for the other twelve). The right answer is – every woman wants to get her own way.[164]

Her *Music for Strings, Trumpets and Percussion* was also from 1958, and the Polmic.pl website describes it as having 'ruthless vitality and resilience of life'.[165] Dedicated to conductor Jan Krenz, the premiere took place in the 1959 Warsaw Autumn. The work received first prize in the orchestral division and third prize overall at UNESCO's International Rostrum of Composers in 1960; and in 1961, the piece won Third Prize at the UNESCO International Tribune Competition. Often performed, it has been used for six different ballets staged by European dance companies. In 1965, during the IV Paris Biennale, it was the music for the ballet *Quadrige* by Pierre du Villard; it has also been danced at the Théatres des Hauts de Seine, and by the Nederlands Dans Theater.[166]

Bartók's *Music for Strings, Percussion and Celesta* (1936) was among the few pieces of his to be known in Poland in the 1950s.[167] Bacewicz's *Music* nods to Bartók's *Music* by separating the concertante groups and individual instruments, using contrasting string harmonies, and including the celeste in the percussion. As a UNESCO prize-winner, and with an acknowledged tribute to Bartók, the work also has parallels with Lutosławski's *Funeral Music* (1958). Bacewicz scored the five trumpets and percussion as obbligato instruments, with different percussion highlighted in each movement (timpani and celeste in the opener, celeste in the central Adagio, and xylophone in the finale). Dominated by dramatic outbursts on the timpani, the first movement includes excited strings, edgy trumpets, and motor percussion; it is sometimes syncopated and almost jazzy. The expressive centre is the second movement,

---

[164] Synopsis provided by PWM Edition.

[165] See 'Bacewicz, *Music for Strings, Trumpets and Percussion*', *Polmic.pl*: https://bacewicz .polmic.pl/en/music-for-strings-trumpets-and-percussion.

[166] At the time of this writing, there are two versions on YouTube and two CD recordings (Hyperion Records; Anthology of the Royal Concertgebouw Orchestra).

[167] See Timothy Judd's discussion of the piece in 'Bartók's *Music for Strings, Percussion and Celeste*: A Haunting Symmetry', *The Listeners' Club*: https://thelistenersclub.com/2018/10/31/ bartoks-music-for-strings-percussion-and-celesta-a-haunting-symmetry.

with the celeste providing the main colour; the initial ostinato and improvisatory duo for viola and double-bass solo recall their precursors in the 1948 *Concerto for String Orchestra*. The Adagio's non-repetitive structure is one of the most experimental in Bacewicz's output. Shorn of motivic and harmonic character, the closing bars of this movement reach a sense of total desolation. Characteristically, the raw emotion is brushed away with a lively finale; the typically spirited Vivace is the most conventional movement of the three. It is a characteristically lively sonata-rondo; brass sonorities are contrasted with divisi strings, which, unusually, include passing references to earlier movements.

More New Techniques

From 1960, Polish music was among the most vital in Europe; progress was led principally by Lutosławski. He had studied some of the forward-looking methods (such as aleatoricism) and began to include the element of chance from his *Venetian Games* (1961) onwards. His chief works of the 1960s stand out for their precise musical language and clear-cut narratives. Compromising between tradition and the avant-garde, East European composers often liked pluralism, slightly neutralising the musical content. The introduction of twelve-tone ideas changed the course of Polish contemporary music, even though strict serialism was not a regular feature. Instead, elements were absorbed into a general style that managed to avoid some of the sterile over-intellectualism of western academic composition. A leading aspect was what one Polish commentator termed 'sonorism', in which sonorities, colour changes, and unusual timbres became the main features.[168] Initiated in the 1950s in Polish music's avant-garde, several notable Polish composers worked with sonorism. Scholar Józef Michał Chomiński (1906–94) coined the term *sonorystyka*, describing musical exploration of purely sonic phenomena.[169] In the 1960s, this Polish music practice concentrated on tone colour, focussing on the specific characteristics and qualities of timbre, texture, articulation, dynamics and motion, attempting to create freer forms, and gaining latitude from strict serialism. However, Roman Maciejewski (1910–98) later countered with 'there is nothing good

---

[168] Adrian Thomas, 'Sonorism and Experimentalism' in *Polish Music since Symanowski* (Cambridge: Cambridge University Press, 2005), pp. 159–207.

[169] See Zbigniew Granat, '(ii) Sonorism', *Grove Music Online*: https://doi.org/10.1093/gmo/9781561592630.article.2061689.

coming from a composition in which sound prevails over music. The system is decidedly upside-down.'[170]

Bacewicz engaged with the new experiments. Here are her opinions on musical language and her compositional process:

> 5 October 1958
>
> Brother Dearest: Your thoughts on form are all very true. There's only one thing I can't really agree with: that a composer should write from intuition. Consciousness is essential in our work – my opinion at least. And then your reasoning is a little one-sided: you tend to overemphasise form at the detriment of other elements. You're not concerned – or so I understand – with the novelty of musical language, as if expressing your musical idea in a new form immediately resulted in the work's being novel in other ways too – in terms of both harmony and rhythm. How can you be so sure? Other composers in the world are not, and hence all that hunt for completely new ways of creating sound . . . . The whole of music is at a crossroads – that much is clear. I'm too old myself to join those who choose to chase such total novelties. My role is to do what I do more or less well; of course, I don't stand still. And so I'll keep on writing for our old instruments, trying to achieve unified expression by making sure I'm original enough in terms of form and musical language and the choice of instruments. And we'll see what happens – hell knows what. I feel you're young enough – or so I imagine – to be able to invent new things in any sphere. The truth is that you're actually more inventive than I am, even if you might not have really made use of it yet. Think about it![171]

A candid account of her musical opinions and more of her thoughts on composing came a couple of weeks later:

> 23 October 1958
>
> Dear Vitek, . . . Why on earth do you start worrying all of a sudden whether or not a piece is a reflection of reality? Only one thing is certain: a composer cannot think about it while writing music. It's good old Plato who said that it's wrong for an artist to work with anything but his own pleasure on his mind. The later fate of what had been written of one's own pleasure – that's a whole other story. It is my opinion that (if the author is good enough) a work can be a reflection of reality in some sense – yet to be honest, I couldn't care less. I am obsessed with a totally different matter: with how people attach too much attention to themselves and their actions. I'm dreaming of writing a book about it, a book I know I'll never write . . . As to our musical discussion: there is an argument for the dodecaphonists, for the possibility of writing beautiful music

---

[170] Maciejewski, *Ruch Muzyczny* 1971, as cited in the *Polish Music Journal* no. 22, p. 4.

[171] Bacewicz (5 October 1958) in 'Letters of Grażyna Bacewicz and Vytautas Bacivičius', pp. 8–9.

within their system. This is an argument by analogy: aren't Bach's Fugues beautiful despite the constraining form? Do you know Berg's Violin Concerto? I'm sure you do. It's beautiful music, even if it's dodecaphonic ... You and I seem to agree and understand each other, yet we think in our different ways. You approach your profession, that of the composer I mean, in a highly romantic fashion ... I treat the job of the composer as carving in stone, and not as a transmission of the sounds of imagination or of inspiration. Most of the world's composers work like bureaucrats, in an ordered way. When their muse abandons them for a while, they do their technical homework ... I would never hold it against anyone that he or she allows a single voice for a longer time. Quite the contrary: it's much better than when all keep on playing, or at least seem to. Then all contrast of colour, register, intensity etc., is gone. Contrast is a very important element of art. For how can one use contrasts when everyone keeps on playing?[172]

While she was not generally interested in explaining her compositional thinking, this is a fair account of it.

Interesting new music was being explored by a younger generation of composers in Poland. Sonorism focussed on tone and sound, using unconventional articulations, varying textures, and colours; it was an approach that Bacewicz dallied with. Sometimes named as Poland's greatest composer, Krzysztof Penderecki (1933–2020) was fascinated with it and he was writing some impressive works around this time.[173] His *Emanations* (1958) – for two string orchestras tuned a minor second apart – won the Second Prize at the Polish Composers Union Young Composers Competition in April 1959, and *The Psalms of David* (premiered in 1959 at the Warsaw Autumn) won First Prize in the Polish Young Composers Competition. In 1960, he wrote *Threnody to the Victims of Hiroshima*, dedicated to the people killed by the first-ever wartime use of an atomic bomb.[174] Musically, it laid the ground for sonorism.

Bacewicz perhaps revealed her awareness of new sounds and new directions in Polish music when she advised her brother in June 1960 to avoid 'outdated' techniques in his compositions. As she stated:

Vitek, ...

While composing, avoid looking at the work of Shostakovich. He is not a good example. He is behind the times. Avoid chromatic scales in the wood[wind].

---

[172] Bacewicz, ibid., pp. 9–10.

[173] See Harrison Smith, 'Krzysztof Penderecki: Acclaimed composer known for his foreboding sound', *Independent* (13 April 2020): www.independent.co.uk/news/obituaries/krzysztof-penderecki-death-composer-music-atonal-poland-film-age-cause-a9440716.html.

[174] Jan Topolski, '*Threnody to the Victims of Hiroshima* – Krzysztof Penderecki', *Culture.pl*: https://culture.pl/en/work/threnody-to-the-victims-of-hiroshima-krzysztof-penderecki.

That's outdated. On the other hand, don't shun long notes in strings, then for example, some movement from the wood[wind], or some noisy brass. You must make a kind of switch in your musical thinking in order to move as far away as possible from your part one. Make it a point of honour to build the following parts completely different one from the other! Don't forget to make your percussion more diversified ....[175]

Characteristically, Bacewicz was continually moving forward in her individual way. Talking about modernising her own musical language, she spoke to writer Jerzy Kosiński about how her *String Quartet No. 6* differed from her previous works:

It is a turn in my oeuvre. It took me a long time to write it, about nine months. I turn in this Quartet to serial music in order to abandon tonality, which has marked my music. In any case, the journey to the Quartet has been an evolution, through Quartet No. 5 and Music for Strings, Trumpet and Percussion.[176]

Part 2: 1960–9

Sonorism – Cellos – Viola Concerto – Picasso Ballet

Bacewicz worked energetically in the early 1960s to produce music, applying the latest compositional ideas: even if the modern approaches were alien, she tackled them head on. This phase was one of stylistic experimentation, including serial techniques, aleatoricism, patchwork collage, and sonorism. Polish music critic Tadeusz Zieliński described Bacewicz's late works in the following way: 'She had an unfolding of style in her last works, she developed different approaches in the architecture and harmony of the music. She employed capricious musical changes.'[177] Musically, there was disintegration of tonality and formal symmetry, extra spacious textures, a more epigrammatic style, and folk traditions were integrated with impressionism. When fellow composer and critic Stefan Kisielewski asked Bacewicz her opinion on the new directions in music, including serialism, she replied:

---

[175] Bacewicz (30 June 1960) in 'Letters of Grażyna Bacewicz and Vytautas Bacivičius', p. 10.

[176] Bacewicz in an interview with Jerzy Kosiński in the Polish journal *Życie Literackie* (16 October 1960), as cited in 'Grażyna Bacewicz, String Quartet No. 6 ', *Polmic.pl*; https:// bacewicz.polmic.pl/en/string-quartet-no-6.

[177] Zieliński, 'Grazyna Bacewicz (1913-69)', *Polish Perspectives*, vol. XVII/10 (October 1974), p. 20: https://archive.org/details/sim_polish-perspectives_1974-10_17_10/mode/2up.

I am very interested, because in music like in everything else, something new must come along from time to time. The technique is very important to me because it provides the necessary rigour and formal technique for the composer. Without this base, improvisation could not be created. As a drawback, I find often the works that have been written all sound quite alike. In the composition I am now writing – the String Quartet No. 6 – I want to maintain certain sections in the serial technique, but by the same token I want to give them a different character. I am not interested in pointillism because I believe the road to be too narrow, but I feel directed by the colouring in sounds and the new rhythms of electronic music.[178]

Her *String Quartet No. 6* was premiered by the Quatuor Parrenin at the Warsaw Autumn Festival in 1960, and it is among her most successful and frequently performed works.[179] It mixes tradition with progressive contemporary techniques, even embracing pointillism.[180] The first movement shows a partial adoption of twelve-note principles. The mercurial scherzo resembles a series of rapid-fire variations. Unconventional harmonics are exploited in the Grave. It ends, tongue-in-cheek, with a scuttling quasi-rondo, fragmented by avant-garde gestures, and with her usual rhythmic *élan*.

It is worth noting that although restrictions on creative freedoms had somewhat eased, state authorities were still keeping a close watch on Polish composers and their creative choices at this time. An opportunity to be open about how progress was being stifled by Soviet control came in a letter she wrote from Italy:

Venice, 8 July 1960
Dear Vitek,

We are leaving Venice for Florence tomorrow morning ... Things are now much worse at home than a year ago – censorship is killing writers and journalists. In the Academy of Fine Arts, for instance, it has been announced that Socialist Realism is again the official style – except that the young people laugh at that and pledge allegiance to abstract art. Even we musicians are being meddled with. It's obviously not a return to Stalinism; still, the hard-liners are gaining ground. It's much more difficult to go abroad than it used to be, and even artists' wages are controlled

---

[178] Bacewicz in Stefan Kisielewski, 'An interview with Grażyna Bacewicz', *Z Muzycznej międzyepoki* (PWM 1965, p. 203) as cited in Rosen, *Grażyna Bacewicz*. Note that Bacewicz showed an open mind, despite having commented on the limitations of this technique in a letter to her brother of 19 October 1957 (quoted previously in this Element).

[179] The Quatuor Parrenin was a French quartet, founded in 1944. The quartet's repertoire was extensive – from Haydn to Bartók. Jacques Parrenin died in 2010.

[180] For further detail, see 'Bacewicz, *String Quartet no 6*', *Polmic.pl*.

to make sure we don't get too much. Letters (from abroad) are opened and read
from time to time. We can't write too much about that from Poland; I can do that
here though ... Some of our 'leaders' and ministers and politicians are scared
shitless of the Soviets, who are once again on the rebound. Still we can't oppose
them too openly because of our unfortunate geography.[181]

Life was clearly difficult in this situation, but she never complained. Two
months later, she wrote:

My Sixth Quartet has been performed at the festival to the annoyance of the old
(e.g. Sikorski) and the surprise of the young. The latter have already thought
I can't go any further, so now they've recognized me all over again. What's
really happened is that the moment has arrived when a composer wants at any
price to leave all that has been behind and starts looking for new things in
music. The young might be a little too weird (as is their right) and the middle
generation are trying to preserve as much music as they can in the "weirdness,"
not just experiments. Anyway, there is no progress without the freedom to
experiment. As a result, I still have the upper hand.[182]

More Remodeling

Pensieri Notturni (Night Thoughts) for chamber orchestra began Bacewicz's
last phase.[183] The piece was premièred on 21 April 1961 at the Venice
Biennale by the Kraków Philharmonic Chamber Orchestra, with another
performance in September at the Warsaw Autumn. It also won an Award
from the Ministry of Culture and Fine Arts. As well as sonorist writing, it
shows traces of the twelve-tone technique. Bacewicz said in her Festival
programme note that she aimed 'to present in an organised way something
that is disorganised in every way, specifically that which is happening in the
mind of a very tired composer'.[184] Suggesting the free association experienced on the verge of sleep, the textures are of sustained background and
fragmentary foreground; it has a magical ending. In terms of purely orchestral
music, it can be regarded as her greatest achievement for the sensitivity of its
sound world. Bacewicz said of the piece:

It might apparently seem ... that this is somehow programme music. But only
apparently ... The distinctive feature of the work ... what happens in it is an
obsessive adherence to certain sounds expanding and narrowing again ...

---

[181] Bacewicz (8 July 1960) in 'Letters of Grażyna Bacewicz and Vytautas Bacivičius', pp. 10–11.

[182] Bacewicz (12 September 1960) in ibid., pp. 11–12.

[183] See 'Bacewicz, *Pensieri Notturni*', *Polmic.pl*: https://bacewicz.polmic.pl/en/pensieri-notturni-
for-chamber-orchestra.

[184] Bacewicz, 'Notes and Letters', Polish Music Center: https://polishmusic.usc.edu/research/
publications/polish-music-journal/vol1no2/grazyna-bacewicz-notes-and-letters/#6.

> The content of the work forced me to treat the instruments in a special way, especially the strings ... The sound material that I use in the composition is not based on any existing system; it has been strictly arranged by myself. The only borrowed element is the principle of non-recurring notes. The work is characterized by an obsessive use of certain notes expanding and returning to their previous states. The composition is meant to be an attempt at conveying something received by the composer perhaps from somewhere. The contents of the composition have made me treat the instruments in a special way, the strings in particular.[185]

Although Bacewicz's compositions don't show any major influence from electronic music, she went to Yugoslavia in 1962 where she visited the new experimental studio for electronic music. On returning to Warsaw, she wrote the *Concerto for Large Symphony Orchestra*, which was premiered at the Warsaw Autumn in September 1962.[186] The four movements – Allegro; Largo; Vivo; Allegro non troppo – are in a slightly revised neo-romantic language. The first and third are vivacious; the Largo is the kernel of the work, with expressive string writing; the finale relates to the grandiose manner of the symphonies.

Cellos

Following on from the *Concerto for Large Symphony Orchestra*, and premiered at the 1963 Warsaw Autumn, the colourful *Cello Concerto No. 2* was inspired by and dedicated to the Spanish cellist Gaspar Cassadó (1879–1966).[187] Modernist sonorities overrule formalism in this piece. Soloist and full ensemble have strong interactions, with the cello dominating the first movement. The percussion instruments have a robust role in this score. In the second movement, the cello is juxtaposed with upper woodwinds and percussion. The soloist stands out in new ways, and the resulting change in texture is engaging through bold gestures. There is a characteristically extroverted finale.

Bacewicz's *Quartet for Four Cellos* was premiered at the 1964 Warsaw Autumn and is an inventive work, drawing interest through a whole kaleidoscope of ideas. With striking originality, Bacewicz avoids the obvious in this unusual instrumental ensemble. Her programme notes state:

---

[185] Bacewicz, an excerpt of personal notes, in *Ruch Muzyczny* 1994, No. 1, as cited in *Pensieri notturni*, PWM Edition: https://pwm.com.pl/en/wypozyczenia/utwory-wg-kategorii/publi kacja/pensieri-notturni,bacewicz-grazyna,10530,hirelibrary.html.

[186] Bacewicz, '*Concerto for Large Symphony Orchestra*', Polmic.pl: https://bacewicz.polmic.pl /en/concerto-for-orchestra.

[187] See 'Bacewicz, *Cello Concerto No 2*', Polmic.pl: https://bacewicz.polmic.pl/en/concerto-no -2-for-cello-and-orchestra.

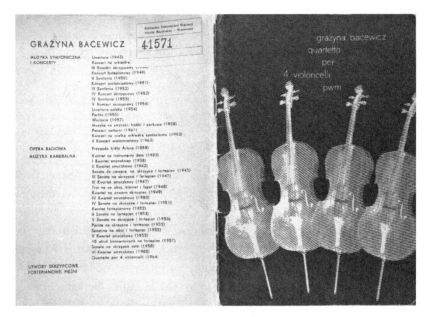

Figure 14 *Quartet for Four Cellos*, PWM Edition

> In bringing together four cellos, I was drawn to the richness of its sound
> matter. When working on the piece … I came to the conclusion that an
> ensemble of four is an inexhaustible treasure for a contemporary composer.
> The concept of the piece forced me to largely reject some of the elements of
> playing [that are] most characteristic of the cello like, for example, broad
> *cantilena*.[188]

Breaking with traditional form, there are just two movements: Narrazione
and Riflessioni. The latter movement includes a short, gigue-like figuration
in 6/8, which is one of Bacewicz's long-standing textures in final movements. In a visceral language, she created a fascinating variety of sonorities
by using a compendium of string techniques. Listening to the preparation to
record this piece on the Ambache Chamber Music CD (2016), grinning from
ear to ear, my husband observed, 'it's like four elephants at a waterhole': he
was referring to the benign quality of elephants. The *Guardian* described it
as 'brilliantly dense, scurrying',[189] and *Planet Hugill* wrote: 'it is an intense
piece, full of dark sonorities and spiky harmonies. It is a tough piece with an
edgy atmosphere and sense of mystery, all-in-all rather terrific.'[190]

---

[188] Bacewicz, note in the Programme of the 6th Warsaw Autumn Festival as cited in 'Bacewicz,
Quartet for 4 Cellos', *Polmic.pl*: https://bacewicz.polmic.pl/en/quartet-for-4-cellos.
[189] Molleson, *Guardian* (2 March 2017).   [190] *Planet Hugill* (31 March 2017).

Patching and Self-Borrowing

Inkrustacje (Incrustations)[191] for horn and ensemble and the *Trio for Oboe, Harp and Percussion* – both written in 1965 – use the same musical material, but with different instrumentation.[192] The middle movement of *Inkrustacje* includes a quotation of the solo part from the *Intermezzo* of the 1955 *Partita*. In 1965, Bacewicz wrote to French horn player Wiesław Moczulski about *Inkrustacje*:

> [B]esides the French horn – the solo instrument – there are only five people: the flute, harp, violin, cello and double-bass. Seldom do we hear the percussion instr.: the gong and two legni, these should be handled by any of the 5 perform-ers accompanying the French horn, that is, by that person who has a pause at that particular moment. This should be determined before distributing the parts. For example, at the beginning of the I movement, the gong should be struck by the flautist or the violinist (this must be written into their part). The part for the harp is quite difficult. In the places marked *sul ponticello*, the strings must really play *sul ponticello* – the same applies to the places marked *con legno*.[193]

The *Trio*'s first performance only took place in 1974 in Bennington College, Vermont, USA, and the players included Marta Ptaszyńska (b. 1943, percus-sionist). Ptaszyńska was a Warsaw composer colleague who later taught at Bennington – probably the reason for the premiere there. Bacewicz explores the atmospheric possibilities of this singular combination of instruments, creat-ing an unusual soundscape. Effects include swirling glissandi from the harp, a poignant oboe line, plus the motley sounds of the various percussion instru-ments. A curious piece, it was described by the *Guardian* as 'eerie',[194] and the musicians recording for the Ambache CD thought it 'strange', but went with it, trusting the composer. Planet Hugill noted:

> Bacewicz uses the slightly unusual combination of instruments to create some spare yet transparent textures. Still rather neo-classical in style, the work is more intense than some of the earlier pieces, with the oboe as the protagonist. The final movement is marked *Giocoso* but it is still spare and very intense. A wonderful and rather imaginative piece.[195]

Bacewicz also completed a ballet during these years, and her light-hearted one-act *Esik in Ostende* received its first performance at the Poznań Opera

---

[191] See M. Gasiorowska note to 'Bacewicz, *Incrustations* for horn and chamber ensemble', PWM Edition: https://pwm.com.pl/en/sklep/publikacja/incrustations,grazyna-bacewicz,11537,shop .html.

[192] See 'Bacewicz, *Trio for Oboe, Harp and Percussion*', *Polmic.pl*: https://bacewicz.polmic.pl/en/ trio-for-oboe-harp-and-percussion.

[193] Bacewicz to Moczulski (1965), as cited in 'From Notes and Letters of Grażyna Bacewicz', Polish Music Center.

[194] Molleson, *Guardian*, op. cit.   [195] *Planet Hugill*, op. cit.

House in 1964.[196] She then composed a *Cantata* for choir and orchestra, commissioned by the Jagiellonian University of Kraków to celebrate its 600th anniversary; the famous astronomer Nicolaus Copernicus (1473–1543) was a student there in 1491–2. The libretto came from the poem *Acropolis* by the Kraków student Stanisław Wyspiański (1869–1907; unofficially known as the Fourth Polish Bard).[197] The *Cantata*'s premiere was on 10 May 1964, and it is a solemn piece of music, befitting such a celebration.

More Musical Abundance

The year 1965 was a remarkably creative one for Bacewicz by any standards. She completed the *Divertimento* for strings, *Musica Sinfonica in Tre Movimenti*, *String Quartet No. 7*, *Violin Concerto No. 7*, *Piano Quintet No. 2*, and *Small Triptych* for piano. At the 1965 Stockholm premiere of the *Musica Sinfonica in Tre Movimenti*, the composer was given a standing ovation.[198] The Dialogo middle movement of this work has a dramatic interaction of high woodwinds (or string ensemble) with low growling ostinato on brass, percussion, and strings, and is followed by a playful, *giocoso* finale.[199] While Bacewicz said that the aleatoric technique didn't interest her much, this music shows some use of the controlled use of chance. Of the new features in her music in this piece, Stefan Kisielewski wrote:

> [T]he traditional subject matter or motivic material is abandoned and replaced by a tangle of instrumental lines conducted in a completely different manner; the work's texture and orchestration are entirely new, unusually enriched and varied; an extremely colourful instrumentation and its incessantly varied pulsation fascinates the listener; there is no trace of the former homogeneous, clear-cut … and vigorous rhythms of Bacewicz's earlier compositions. Of the utmost importance for me, however, is a new kind of emotionalism, the new expression which pervades the piece: a Rousselian monumentalism of the four symphonies is replaced by a very direct and spontaneous expressionism.[200]

---

[196] Lech Terpiłowski's ballet scenario is based on Tadeusz Boy-Żeleński's 'Esik's Day in Ostend', a tale that makes generous allusion to words of admiration for the charms of Vienna's nightlife by (publicist/music publisher) Ferdynand Hoesick (1867–1941). See biography of 'Ferdynand Hoesick', *The Fryderyk Chopin Institute*: https://en.chopin.nifc.pl/chopin/persons/detail/id/608.

[197] See 'Stansław Wyspiański', *Culture.pl*: https://culture.pl/en/artist/stanislaw-wyspianski.

[198] 'Bacewicz, *Musica sinfonica in tre movimenti*', *Polmic.pl*: https://bacewicz.polmic.pl/en/musica-sinfonica-in-tre-movimenti-2.

[199] Note that both the English Contemporary Ballet Company and the Australian Ballet Company have choreographed this work. The Australian Ballet choreographed it as the accompaniment to *Threshold* in 1969, 1970, and 1972, in Sydney, Melbourne, Adelaide, Brisbane, Perth, and Canberra.

[200] Stefan Kisielewski, *Ruch Muzyczny*, no. 17 (1965) as cited in Bacewicz, *Musica sinfonia in tre movimenti*, PWM Edition: https://pwm.com.pl/en/sklep/publikacja/musica-sinfonica-in-tre-movimenti,grazyna-bacewicz,10527,shop.html.

Arguably Bacewicz's most successful concerto, her *Violin Concerto No. 7* won the Prize of the Belgian Government and the Gold Medal at the Queen Elizabeth International Competition.[201] No longer playing herself, the premiere (in January 1966) was given by soloist Augustín León Ara (b. 1936), with the Belgian Radio and Television Symphony Orchestra at the Grande Salle de Palais de Beaux-Arts, Brussels. Various different people have described the music as visionary, eerie, exotic, quixotic, allusive, improvisatory, and ecstatic in flavour.[202]

In the first two movements there is a gratifying balance between the violin and the richly scored orchestra (soli and divisi strings). Including a reference to her *Partita*'s Intermezzo (1955), the lyrical, central Largo is searching and questioning; the dashing and virtuosic finale returns to her much favoured 6/8 time signature, but with destabilising rhythmic disruptions. There is much use of the high register, with strings using this opportunity for enormous glissandi. Simple duets contrast with complex contrapuntal writing. The solo/tutti relationship is one of almost equal partners; there are many concertante groups. International violinist Andrzej Grabiec said this work belongs among the masterpieces of the violin repertoire.[203]

Commissioned by Władysław Szpilman, the *Piano Quintet No. 2* was composed in 1965, but only premiered in 1972 in Salzburg.[204] It was performed by the Warsaw Piano Quintet, founded by Szpilman, and included violinist Bronisław Gimpel (1911–79) and violist Stefan Kamasa (b. 1930). This *Second Quintet* shows great textural contrasts, experimenting with colour and timbre in string writing. The initial Moderato Allegro (– Molto Allegro) begins gently and develops an interplay of motifs around the intervals of a fifth and a second; glissandi appear frequently in both piano and strings. Rising and falling seconds grow in importance in the dark Larghetto (which includes material from her violin *Partita*). The piano has a healthy dialogue with the strings in the dance-like Allegro giocoso.[205]

---

[201] For information about the Queen Elizabeth Competition: https://concoursreineelisabeth.be/en/about.

[202] See 'Bacewicz, *Violin Concerto no. 7*', *Polmic.pl*: https://bacewicz.polmic.pl/en/concerto-no-7-for-violin-and-orchestra. This concerto is included on the 'Bacewicz Violin Concertos 1, 3 and 7' CD, Joanna Kurkowicz (violin), Lukasz Borowicz (conductor), Polish Radio Symphony Orchestra, Chandos 10533 (2009).

[203] Andrzej Grabiec cited in 'Bacewicz Biography', Polish Music Center.

[204] Szpilman had also premièred the *Quintet No. 1*.

[205] Bacewicz was increasingly patching-in previous ideas at this time. Earlier material is used again; for example, in the Larghetto slow movement of the *Concerto for Two Pianos* (1966). Intense, dissonant, and ambitious, this is a powerful work, and there's no let-up in the finale, which even sounds quite crotchety in places. The proportions of the three movements are still elegantly spacious, while filled in with a collage-like method. Some critics have thought the

The three short piano pieces *Maly Tryptyk* (Small Triptych) were dedicated to Regina Smendzianka, who premiered them in Helsinki in 1965. Smendzianka said that they have some fascinating dynamic and aural effects due to a most interesting use of the sustaining pedal.[206] Highly focused miniatures, they are an exploration of colours characterised by an atmosphere of fantasy and subjectivity. The piano tone is of the utmost importance; there are wide leaps and a partiality for sevenths and ninths. Regarding the suggestion that Bacewicz was recycling for want of ideas, there are plenty of new thoughts and methods here.

The *Divertimento* for string orchestra was commissioned by conductor Karol Teutch (1921–92), and he led the National Philharmonic Chamber Orchestra in its November 1966 premiere in Munich.[207] There is a delightful, nimble, graceful opening Allegro. The tritone interval is fundamental to the work, particularly shaping the language of the Adagio, which mixes eerie atmospherics with bald open strings; then the roguish Giocoso sparkles with a variety of ethereal figures. For seven minutes, with brilliant hues, it *diverts*.

Last String Quartet, Gold Medal and *Contradizione*

Written in 1965, Bacewicz's *String Quartet No. 7* was premiered in May 1966 in Łancut by the Bulgarian Dimov Quartet.[208] A September 1966 concert at the Warsaw Autumn included this piece together with Bartók's *Quartet No. 2*, Constantin Iliev's *Fourth Quartet*, and Vasil Kasandjiev's *Perspectives*.

The Polish critic Tadeusz Zieliński described this work as 'a masterpiece of contemporary quartet literature'.[209] Bacewicz combined traditional formal ideas with avant-garde techniques, conveying new possibilities in the genre. She used free serial technique to bring elements of colour to the fore, plus a whole new repertoire of sounds – an engaging sequence of murmuring and skittering effects, glissandi, and clusters. The central Grave is austere, grim, spectral, and occasionally brutal, with a jaunty violin theme making a surprising ending. Playful, with an irregular rhythmic pulse, the final Con vivezza is an

---

patchwork technique indicates lack of fresh ideas; they might consider how many eighteenth-century composers 'recycled' their musical themes and designs.

[206] Cited in Maciejewski, *Twelve Polish Composers*, pp. 73–4.

[207] Bacewicz, *Divertimento*, Polmic.pl: https://bacewicz.polmic.pl/en/divertimento-for-string-orchestra;
    Bacewicz, *Divertimento* at PWM Edition: https://pwm.com.pl/en/wypozyczenia/utwory-wg-kategorii/publikacja/divertimento,bacewicz-grazyna,11183,hirelibrary.htm.

[208] See 'Bacewicz, *String Quartet No. 7*', *Polmic.pl*: https://bacewicz.polmic.pl/en/string-quartet-no-7.

[209] Zieliński, cited in Rosen, *Grażyna Bacewicz*.

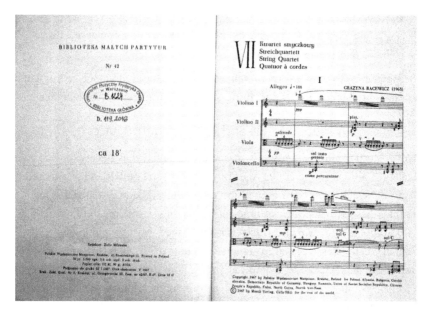

Figure 15 *String Quartet No. 7,* PWM

ingenious, catchy rondo. It is an effective piece, which was internationally acclaimed, even though the musical atmosphere sometimes borders on the unhinged. Lutosławski wrote:

> The String Quartet No. 7 is new evidence of the use of certain possibilities that have been hidden in this type of an ensemble, but which have never been utilized. From the time of Bartók very few composers have written in the same manner as Bacewicz who was able to penetrate the secrets of the string quartet.[210]

Following this, her next composition, *Contradizione,* was written in 1966 and commissioned by the Hopkins Center in Hanover, New Hampshire, USA.[211] Here are the programme notes she wrote for the 1967 Warsaw Autumn Festival:

> A piece for a fifteen-member chamber ensemble completed last December. The choice of the instruments was not accidental, for the fundamental element: juxtaposition of all kinds of musical contradictions ... depended on the instruments used in the work. Obviously, the juxtaposition of contra-dictions was not an end in itself. The overriding goal was to create, out of these contradictory elements, a piece that would not only 'withstand' these

---

[210] Lutoslawski, cited in ibid.
[211] See 'Bacewicz, *Contradizione'*, *Polmic.pl*: https://bacewicz.polmic.pl/en/contraddizione-for-chamber-orchestra.

juxtapositions of the musical material, but would also be able – thanks to its structure – to bind them together so closely that they would produce a fresh artistic experience as a result.[212]

Composing for small forces enabled her to feature individual instrumental colours; motivic fragments dart from one group of instruments to another.

Writing Stories and Talking about Music

Alongside her musical activities, it should be noted that Bacewicz was also a talented author. In the 1960s, she completed several novels and short stories, many of which have been quoted in this volume. The only collection of her writings issued was the volume of anecdotes entitled *Znak szczególny* (*A Distinguishing Mark*), which was published by Czytelnik in 1970.[213] Contained in this collection is an account of a conversation between Boulanger and Bacewicz, where the young Pole describes finding the life of a woman composer very taxing: being a wife, mother, housewife, and creative was impossible. Boulanger replied that in order to succeed in this essentially masculine world, there was no time for self-pity and weak moments.[214] (The 'motorek' must have been her saving grace.)[215]

Some of Bacewicz's writings are autobiographical (as just noted), many are entertaining, and she is happily amused by her own failings. Worldwide, people would ask her to tell them the way, despite her admitting to having no sense of direction. Even in comparatively small Warsaw, some days she couldn't find her own street![216] She described the rude, middle-aged neighbour who turned the radio on full blast to cover the sound of her composing at the piano: 'some bloody lunatic who instead of playing Chopin or some Viennese waltzes was abusing the piano by causing it to produce a lot of disjointed discords'.[217] On tour in India, playing Szymanowski's *Fountain of Arethusa*, during the voluptuous arpeggios and trills of the *Cantilena,* she was disturbed by a strange shimmering noise from the audience: her Indian friend explained afterwards that they loved it so much they wanted it repeated and were displeased when she took no notice.[218]

Bacewicz did not like being interviewed or talking about her music; one story described how difficult she found it. Her reply to persistent questioning on

---

[212] Bacewicz, programme note in the 1967 Warsaw Autumn Festival Programme as cited in 'Works in detail, *Contradizione', Polmic.pl:* https://bacewicz.polmic.pl/en/contraddizione-for-chamber-orchestra.

[213] The English translation by Anna Clarke and Andrew Cienski was published in 2004.

[214] As recounted in 'Should a Composer Have Children?', *A Distinguishing Mark*, p. 21.

[215] See the description of Bacewicz's 'moterek' in the Introduction of this Element.

[216] 'Epilogue S.O.S.' *A Distinguishing Mark*, p. 95.   [217] 'That's Incredible', ibid., p. 56.

[218] Several stories in *A Distinguishing Mark*.

composing by a member of the public was, 'Should I disclose to everyone my most private matters?' Then, a woman wanted to know the meaning of the piece she had just played – to which Bacewicz answered that the piece had no meaning, it was purely musical. The questioner continued with asking about what motivated a composer. After a (colourful) private curse, she said that the interior motivations that lead a composer to start writing a piece are very complex, involved, and intangible. As her interlocutor continued, the response described the germinating of ideas taking weeks or months.[219]

Her writings show an understanding of human nature in a wide range of circumstances, from war, composers, psychological problems, to criminal events. She penned four novels (sold, but not published); a television play (performed on Polish TV in 1969);[220] the stories and essays, and she also wrote for the theatre, radio, and films. She composed incidental music for Shakespeare's *Macbeth* and *Troilus and Cressida* (both 1960), Krasiński's *The Undivine Comedy* (1959), Suchowo-Kobylin's *The Case* (1961), Słowacki's *Balladyna* (1965), the film music to Konopnicka's 1896 children's book *About Little Mary and the Dwarfs*, and several films for children.

A Sketch – Concerto for Two Pianos and Orchestra – Viola Concerto

Other compositions from the fast-paced year of 1966 include *Esquisse* (Sketch) for organ, and the *Concerto for Two Pianos and Orchestra*. The French organist, composer, and pedagogue Jean Guillou (1930–2019) asked Bacewicz to write a piece for him, and the short *Sketch* (literally – 3 minutes) is dedicated to him. In complete contrast, the *Concerto for Two Pianos* (1966) is one of her most dynamic and dashing compositions. Notably spontaneous, it has stringent harmonies and is at times brutal. The instrumental construction is from Polish clusters and blocks of voluptuous sounds to create barbaric and percussive effects.[221] Although the language is ultra-modern, the form is almost classical; the central Larghetto is the soul of the work.

Bacewicz also had thoughts of a new viola concerto.[222] Up to this time, the Polish repertoire for the viola was relatively small: from composers of neighbouring countries, there were works with orchestra by Benda, Wranitsky, Martinů, Enescu, Škerjanc, Sobanski, Seiber, and Bartók. Stefan Kamasa,

---

[219] 'Scandal', ibid., p. 15.

[220] Awarded a distinction in a competition organised by the Teatr Aterneum, Warsaw; see 'Bacewicz, Writer', *Polmic.pl*: https://bacewicz.polmic.pl/en/writer.

[221] Clusters are chords of adjacent notes; the technique was notably used by Penderecki in *Threnody to the Victims of Hiroshima*, 1960.

[222] See 'Bacewicz, *Concerto for Viola*', *Polmic.pl*: https://bacewicz.polmic.pl/en/concerto-for-viola-and-orchestra.

who had played with the legendary Warsaw Quintet for twenty-three years, asked Bacewicz to write a viola concerto for him:

> I asked Grażyna to write a Concerto, a virtuoso work which would explore the noble tone of the viola. To my intense joy 'the first lady of Polish music' agreed immediately. But, unfortunately, the first sketches of my Concerto she very naughtily incorporated into her seventh *Violin Concerto*. I waited patiently for 3 years and in June 1967 I received a letter from Grażyna in which she said 'There must be a jinx on your Concerto. Everything was going smoothly when I suddenly received an urgent offer to write a composition for the opening of the Havana Festival. Reluctantly, I put aside your Concerto – though not for always. Besides, I believe you did not intend to play it before 1969. It will be ready in a year.'
>
> As always, Grażyna kept her promise. It was to be her last completed work before her sudden and premature death. The *Concerto*, which is dedicated to me, is the favourite in my concert repertoire. I gave its first performance in the Warsaw Autumn 1969. The rousing ovation with many curtain calls from the unusually warm Warsaw audience I interpreted partly as a tribute to the composer. I have played it with the Berlin Philharmonic Orchestra, with the Royal Liverpool Philharmonic Orchestra in Paris, and in several cities in the Soviet Union. Polish critics founded an annual prize for the best performance at the Warsaw Autumn called the Orpheus Prize. I am rather proud of the fact that my performance earned me this honour.
>
> Beside Sir William Walton's Concerto, I favour and love Grażyna's Concerto best. It is a work in three traditional movements. The first is maintained in free sonata form and opens with a slow introduction. The viola solo, kept rather dark in colour, is heard for the first time rising above a background of the suppressed thunder of the percussion section. The aural effect is shattering! The melodic line is rather atonal, yet very Bergian and beautiful. It is, however, the second movement which makes, in my opinion, the biggest impression on the audience. It is, perhaps, one of the most lyrical movements ever written by Grażyna. The viola (*con sordino*/muted) combines with harp and celeste in mysterious music-making full of longing for warmth, just to fade away and give room to the orgiastic finale, overflowing in rhythmic excitement and a very Boulezian choice of instruments. I even sense the distinct influence of Lutosławski's orchestration (*Venetian Games*) in the scherzo-like last movement.[223]

The Festival of Contemporary Music in Havana commissioned the work *In una parte* for orchestra,[224] which Bacewicz completed before returning to the *Viola Concerto*. This piece opened the Festival and was first performed by the Havana Symphony Orchestra in 1967. In the extrovert expressionist tradition, it

---

[223] Stefan Kamasa, cited in Maciejewski, *Twelve Polish Composers*, p. 76.
[224] See 'Bacewicz, *In una parte*', *Polmic.pl:* https://bacewicz.polmic.pl/en/in-una-parte-for-orchestra.

is made up of violent clashes and abrupt contrasts of orchestral musical ideas; the tone is blustering and aggressive. It shows features of Bacewicz's late style, including persistent single-note reiterations, harmony built of perfect fifths and tritones, and a fluctuation between forward motion and sudden stasis.

Ballet: *Desire*

Throughout this period, Bacewicz continued with her public work. She was again a jury member for the International Violin Competition in Naples in 1967, was Chair of the jury at the Wieniawski International Violin Competitions (Poznań) in 1967, and a jury member for the 1968 International Quartet Competition in Budapest. She also served as the first female vice-president of the Polish Composers' Union (1960–69) and was Professor of Composition at Warsaw Conservatory (from 1966).[225] Characteristically, these final years were also marked by creative productivity and some interesting new commissions. Not long before her death, Bacewicz was persuaded by librettist Mieczysław Bibrowski to compose the music for a ballet by Picasso – *Pożądanie* (Desire). She wrote:

> I'm writing a full-evening Ballet in honour of Picasso – with his knowledge and consent. The libretto is based on Picasso's play, but we go far away from it. This rather uninteresting play is just a pretext . . . the plan: completely new things on stage and a new approach to dance.[226]

Thus, she came again to the genre of ballet, and for six months in 1968 she composed a work based on Picasso's *Desire Trapped by the Tail*. Picasso's surrealist play had been conceived in 1941 during the occupation of Paris as an act of resistance; it refers to his indecision on whether to remain in Paris or to emigrate during the Nazi occupation of France. It is about overcoming fear: the characters are allegorical and concerned with hunger, cold, and love. Among the parts, 'The Big Foot' personifies Picasso, and the 'Thin and Fat Terrors' represent

---

[225] According to the Polmic.pl website, Bacewicz faced a difficult challenge as Vice-President and Chair of the Polish Composers Union. Just before the Board meeting on 11 March 1968, Zygmunt Mycielski arrived with a draft letter asking Board members to express support for the position adopted by the Extraordinary General Assembly of the Warsaw Branch of the Polish Writers' Union regarding the 'March events' (students and others protesting against the communist regime, which were suppressed by the security forces). Bacewicz, together with members of her Board, refused to support this, while also avoiding any recriminations from authorities. See 'Bacewicz, Final Years', *Polmic.pl*: https://bacewicz.polmic.pl/en/final-years.

[226] Bacewicz (1969), cited in '*Desire*', *Polmic.pl*. Note that in order to compose this ballet for the Grand Theatre in Warsaw, Bacewicz requested a sabbatical leave from her position as Professor at the Warsaw Conservatory in 1967. The Rektor, Teodor Zalewski, granted her permission for temporary absence (from 1.X.67 to 30.IX.68). This was a special authorisation for a full professor – the professional position was kept for her.

Figure 16 *Pożądanie / Desire* score, Act 1, p. 108

the fear which took hold of Picasso and all of France. The structure of the two-act ballet resembles a modern divertissement, with scenes alternating between grotesque and surrealistic. Her score gives a glimpse of the detail of her ideas.

Work on the ballet was interrupted by a demanding schedule of travelling to international competition juries and performances of her music. The piece was almost finished in December 1968 when her duties as Vice-President of the Polish Composers Union took over: in this role, she accepted an invitation from the Armenian government to their Polish Music Decade Celebrations Festival. The last known photo of Bacewicz shows her there in December 1968. Unfortunately, she caught Asian flu while travelling and her health deteriorated.

Before departing, she did something she had never done before: she left detailed instructions for the completion of the last four minutes of *Desire*. It is impossible to know whether this was a premonition or not. Despite good medical care, she never saw the ballet, as she died on 17 January 1969; with her unrelenting commitment and activity, Wanda seemed to think that she had worked herself to death. The musical world was saddened – Shostakovich and Boulanger sent letters of condolence. The ballet was completed according to her instructions by the conductor-composer Bogusław Madey (1932–2004), but the Grand Theatre of Warsaw did not accept the ending, and the first performance (18 March 1973) ended on the last note that Bacewicz had originally written. Wanda noted that:

The order that had always prevailed in her work took the upper hand even at this critical moment. The decision of the Grand Theatre, I felt, was justified. Nothing had to be added to my sister's music.[227]

Valediction

The music of Bacewicz's last five years balanced the old and the new with her personal approach. She maintained her stylistic individuality in the problematic post-war decades partly through her long-standing relationship with folk music. While she disliked being regarded as a woman composer, she sustained this uncommon position with strength. Her music has lasted, thanks to her energy, honesty, subtlety, and instinctive and impulsive qualities. She always seemed to be 'on purpose'.

Her publisher PWM reported a decline in popularity of her music after her death, but say that more recently she has been top of their list for domestic sales of sheet music.[228] Performers, academics, and musicologists have raised her profile, and anniversaries have further boosted interest. Bacewicz provided a model that has made it possible for other Polish women to maintain their musical activities. In a tribute to Bacewicz, Witold Rudziński noted that:

> We have to admire the enthusiasm with which she absorbed new currents, and at the same time her instinct, which prompted her what to include in her arsenal of achievements, and what to refuse in order not to lose that which is the most important for every artist in the end: their own artistic countenance, own artistic individuality.[229]

From studies with Sikorski, via Boulanger and the French neoclassical influence, to her involvement with contemporary idioms, she always had a sense of order. She had unique imaginative abilities, a fine sense of balancing energy and poignancy; and she wrote at a highly impressive rate. After Szymanowski's influence, she evolved in her own unique way and created the next great appreciation of Polish music. Tadeusz Baird wrote a eulogy in the *Polish Music Quarterly*:

> Polish music was plunged into mourning at the loss of one of its eminent artists. Death struck quickly and unexpectedly. Just a few days earlier Grażyna Bacewicz had been seen at the concert in the National

---

[227] Wanda Bacewicz, as cited in Rosen, *Grażyna Bacewicz*.
[228] Author's correspondence with PWM.
[229] Rudziński (1969), as cited in Katarzyna Bartos, 'The National Element in Grazyna Bacewicz's Music', *Meakultura*.

Philharmonic Hall. Listening to her future plans, seeing her so full of life and her usual captivating charm, who could have guessed that she was already marked with the stigma of death? The life's work of Bacewicz is imposing in quantity and diversity. She has written works in almost all the existing musical forms. She wrote plays, a novel and some short stories. She was a superb craftsman. This fact emerges upon closer analysis of any of her scores and upon listening to even a fragment of any of her works.

But the hallmark of her composing technique is not technical virtuosity. Her music is most genuine, sincere, passionate and very dramatic; it is deeply experienced art and very profound. An effort to label her work, to divide it into different periods, proved totally unsuccessful. Her neo-classical tendencies were actually her very personal excursions, which were overcome to vanish entirely. How typical of this rebel was her clash with dodecaphonic music. One need only look at her fourth *String Quartet* to understand the effect that trend had on her creative development.

The artist enlarged her *metiér* by new elements, but retained her Slavonic individuality. Her sudden death stopped her hand on the very last page of *Desire*, which was to be her last composition. The work of Grażyna Bacewicz, the pride of Polish music and a valuable contribution to the music of our time, lives and speaks with a living voice of art. Therein lay the victory of creative genius over death.[230]

Conclusion

'Can a woman be a full-blooded composer? Should a woman composer get married? Should a woman composer have children? I used to run away from these questions, but I will tell you: a woman with composing abilities can be a serious composer, can marry, have children, travel, have adventures.' This was Bacewicz's opinion, as expressed in one of her short stories.[231]

Grażyna Bacewicz was one of the most important figures in Polish music in the first half of the twentieth century. Witold Lutosławski wrote a fine acknowledgement of her achievements in the foreword to Judith Rosen's monograph, where, as well as appreciating her compositional skills, he noted her personal qualities of humanity and integrity. Talking about her recording, *The Polish Violin* in 2019, violinist Jennifer Pike described the Polish character as having seriousness, intensity, nostalgia, and melancholy.[232] Bacewicz's music fits with this.

---

[230] Baird, *Ruch muzyczny* No. 7 (1969), as cited in Rosen, *Bacewicz: Her Life and Works*, Polish Music History, 1984, p. 39.

[231] Bacewicz, 'Should a Composer Have Children?', *A Distinguishing Mark*, p. 21.

[232] See Katherine Cooper, 'Jennifer Pike on *The Polish Violin*', *Presto Classical*, 10 January 2019: www.prestomusic.com/classical/articles/2438–interview-jennifer-pike-on-the-polish-violin.
    In October 2021, Chandos released *The Polish Violin* No. 2 (CHAN 20189), which includes Pike's performance of Bacewicz's *Polish Caprice* for violin as well as works by Szymanowski and Poldowski.

Her music has stood the test of time, thanks to her stylistic coherence and individual expression.

Defining a lineage around Bacewicz is not simple, as she was an independent. She grew up in a musical environment, in a country with a strong musical tradition. Among her numerous contemporaries at the Łòdż Music Academy, none reached the same level of public acknowledgement as she did.[233] Reportedly, in teaching, she spoke privately with most of her students, and the Łòdż Academy does not now hold a list of who studied with her. The broad range of her activities is impressive; this multiplicity may be a part of her not being known for one unique skill.

Her father, her first teacher, gave her a great love of, and commitment to music; then Helena Kijeńska delivered a theoretical grounding, in Łòdż. Karol Szymanowski was an inspiration, as her advisor and teacher in Warsaw, and first-class experiences on the violin came from friendship with David Oistrakh and learning with Carl Flesch. Studies in Paris suited her sense of form and clarity in composing, as well as the opportunity to work with Nadia Boulanger (another pioneering woman). Important colleagues included Grzegorz Fitelberg and Stefan Kisielewski, and friends such as Władisław Szpilman and Stefan Kamasa, who commissioned work from her. Her other contributions to Polish musical life included serving as Vice-President to the Polish Composers Union, and co-founding of the Warsaw Autumn Festival.

Some 150 of Bacewicz's compositions are published by Polskie Wydawnictwo Muzyczne (PWM).[234] Her biography on the PWM website acknowledges her broadly:

> Grażyna Bacewicz's creative output is extremely rich and varied, ranging from solo miniatures and chamber works to symphonies and concertos with solo instruments, songs, cantatas, ballets and a radio opera. She also wrote music for film and theatrical performances. Successful literary work was another facet of this comprehensively oriented creative personality, open and sensitive to all the manifestations of the world around her. The numerous prizes and distinctions with which she was honoured are an expression of recognition for her titanic work and artistic and compositional achievements as a consequence of which she deservedly gained a reputation as the greatest Polish woman composer – an outstanding figure of our century's music.[235]

---

[233] Although he belonged to a different generation of composers, Henryk Górecki (1933–2010) followed Bacewicz to wider European success, notably with his *Symphony No. 3* (1978).

[234] https://pwm.com.pl/en/search/?q=bacewicz&autorid=&title=&kryteria=wszedzie&numer=.

[235] 'Biography – Grażyna Bacewicz', PWM website: https://pwm.com.pl/en/kompozytorzy_i_au torzy/4782/grazyna-bacewicz/index.html.

The state-owned recording company Polskie Nagrania Muza made a long list of recordings of her music, starting in 1932, with a piano *Toccata* played by Eliza Wasiek. Bacewicz is well served in the contemporary CD world, and her music appears in various recording company catalogues, including Chandos, Deutsche Grammophon, Dux, Naxos, Hyperion, and many others. In print, there is a major life and works biography by Małgorzata Gąsiorowska (PWM Edition). The British musicologist Adrian Thomas has written notably about her chamber and orchestral music, and online materials about her life and work, including Judith Rosen's monograph, can be found at the Polish Music Center, University of Southern California.[236]

Surveying Bacewicz's music in more detail, her seven string quartets occupy a central position in twentieth-century quartet-writing and have been described as an alternative biography of the composer. There are two complete recorded sets of these quartets – by the Lutosławski String Quartet (Naxos) and the Silesian String Quartet (Chandos). Selected as Gramophone's Recording of the Month in July 2016, the magazine's review of the Silesian Quartet's recording endorsed their importance:

> Bacewicz's Quartets are essential listening, and the Silesian Quartet really give the impression of having lived with them. They approach the cycle as a unity. Chandos captures the Silesian Quartet in a lucid, atmospheric recorded sound that's gutsy without being hectoring ... the assurance, insight and finish of this particular set, make it feel like a landmark – an assertion of this music's place at the heart of the twentieth-century quartet repertoire.[237]

In addition Bacewicz's contribution to the violin repertoire was exceptional, and her five sonatas for violin and piano are distinguished works, full of character and instrumental ideas. Her compositions for larger forces also were significant: writing four symphonies was no mean feat! Premiered on 18 June 1950 during a General Assembly of the Polish Composers' Union, her magnum opus, the *Concerto for String Orchestra* (1948), will probably continue to be her most popular work.[238]

Compositionally, Bacewicz was not so much an avant-gardist as an explorer who followed her instincts and found her own path. Terms associated with her music include folklorism, neoclassicism, neoromanticism, and

---

[236] See Rosen, *Grażyna Bacewicz:* https://polishmusic.usc.edu/research/publications/polish-music-journal/vol5no1/grazyna-bacewicz-life-and-works/. See also the excellent website dedicated to Bacewicz by *Polmic.pl*: https://bacewicz.polmic.pl/en.

[237] R. Bratby, 'Bacewicz String Quartets', *Gramophone* (August 2016): www.gramophone.co.uk/review/bacewicz-string-quartets.

[238] For Stefan Kisielewski's description of the strength of this work, see Section 2 of this Element.

sonorism. These labels have some value if taken as pointers and not restrictive descriptions. Stylistically, she defies categorisation; generalisations don't do her justice. She was an individual who maintained her stylistic independence, while still being part of her time. Her popularity with the Polish people came from her attractive incorporation of folk tunes. Her natural tendency to good craftsmanship led her to write well-constructed works; her bright energy drew attention, and she had an engaging sense of colour.

Her sturdy way with the world enabled her to go on composing and playing through a complex period in Polish history, both during World War II and afterwards in the communist period. As a pioneer, the word 'trailblazer' has been applied to her life and achievements, and the fact that few women had previously been given due credit as composers underlines this point. According to Polish composer Bernadetta Matuszczak (1837–2021), Bacewicz was the first woman composer in Poland to be accepted as an equal by her male peers:

> In Poland, Grażyna opened the way for women composers ... It was difficult for her, but she won; with her great talent, she became famous ... . Afterwards, we had an open path, and nobody was surprised: 'My God, a woman composer again!' Bacewicz had already been there, so the next one also had a right to exist.[239]

National pride in Bacewicz's many achievements has been expressed in various ways. The Bacewicz family is important to the city of Łòdż, who named their Music School the *Academy Grażyna i Kiejstuta Bacewiczów w Łodzi*, and there are violin and composition competitions in her name in Łódż. There are streets named after Bacewicz in Łòdż, Warsaw, and Gdańsk, as well as in Konin, Czestochoka, and Bialystock, and schools bearing her name in four different cities, including Koszalin and Warsaw. Bacewicz is one of the seven statues of great Polish musical personalities lining the front of Bydgoszcz Philharmonic Hall. A notable mark of honour, she is buried on the Avenue of the Meritorious in the Powąski Military Cemetery, Warsaw – among the 'deserving ones'.

Readers interested in hearing more of her music can find it on YouTube, Spotify, and on CD. Due recognition will come and appropriate appreciation will grow as we, as performers, communicate how much we relish playing it and include it in our programming. String players who enjoy chamber music will certainly be engaged by her *Quartet for Four Violins*; the fine violin sonatas enriched Polish musical literature impressively. The Polish people are rightly proud of her exceptional music-making. In her story 'An Understanding',

---

[239] Matuszczak cited in 'Bacewicz Biography', Polish Music Center.

Figure 17 Grażyna Bacewicz

Bacewicz wrote of the way audiences were in harmony with her.[240] We need to continue to respond to music by Grażyna Bacewicz, a truly outstanding figure in twentieth-century music.

---

[240] Bacewicz, *A Distinguishing Mark*, p. 51.

Select Bibliography

Books and Articles

Anderson, D. (2004). 'Chamber Music in Early Piano Study: A Guide to Repertoire', DMA dissertation, University of Cincinnati.

Bacewicz, G. (2004). *A Distinguishing Mark*, English translation by A. Clarke & A. Cienski, 3rd ed., Ontario: Krzys Chmiel. Originally published in Polish as *Znak Szczególny*, Warsaw: Czytelnik, 1970.

Elphick, D. (2019). *Music Behind the Iron Curtain: Weinberg and his Polish Contemporaries*, Cambridge: Cambridge University Press.

Gąsiorowska, M. (1999). *Bacewicz*, Krakow: Polskie Wydawnictwo Muzyczne.

Harley, M. A. (1997). 'Bacewicz, Picasso and the Making of *Desire*', *Journal of Musicological Research*, 16(4), 243–81.

Hoffman, E. (1989). *Lost in Translation*, London: Heinemann.

Kirk, N. C. (2001). 'Grażyna Bacewicz and Social Realism', DMA dissertation, University of Washington.

Kisielewski, S. (1964). *Grażyna Bacewicz i jej czasy* (Grażyna Bacewicz and Her Times), Krakow: Polskie Wydawnictwo Muzyczne.

Lang, P. H. and Broder, N. (1966). *Contemporary Music in Europe*, London: Dent.

Maciejewski, B. M. (1976). *Twelve Polish Composers*, London: Allegro Press.

Mills, C. R. (1987). 'Grażyna Bacewicz: A Stylistic Analysis and Evaluation of Selected Keyboard Works', DMA dissertation, University of Northern Colorado.

Paja-Stach, J. (2010). *Polish Music from Paderewski to Penderecki*, Krakow: Musica Iagellonica.

Pendle, K., ed. (2001). *Women and Music: A History*, 2nd ed., Bloomington: Indiana University Press.

Rosen, J. (1984). *Bacewicz, Her Life and Works*, Los Angeles: Friends of Polish Music, University of California.

Ross, A. (2009). *The Rest Is Noise*, New York: Harper Perennial.

Sadie, J. A. and Samuel, R., eds. (1994). *The New Grove Dictionary of Women Composers*, New York: Norton.

Salzman, E. (2002). *Twentieth Century Music: An Introduction*, 4th ed., Upper Saddle River, NJ: Prentice Hall History of Music.

Sendłak, J. (2018). *Z Ogniem – Miłość Grażyny Bacewicz w przededniu wojny*, Warsaw: Skarpa Warszawska.

Shafer, S. G. (1992). *The Contribution of Grażyna Bacewicz (1909–1969) to Polish Music*, Lewiston, NY: Mellon Press.

Shofner, T. L. (1996). 'The Two Piano Quintets of Grażyna Bacewicz: An Analysis of Style and Content', DMA dissertation, University of Wisconsin.

Slonimsky, N. (1994). *Music since 1900*, 5th ed., New York: Macmillan.

Sobkowska, J. (2004). 'Works for Chamber Ensemble with Piano Written Between 1950 and 2000 by Polish Composers: An Annotated Bibliography', DMA dissertation, Florida State University.

Szerszenowicz, J. (2016). *Grażyna Bacewicz – Witraż* (Stained-Glass Window), Akademia Muzyczna im Grażyny I Keijstuta Bacewiczów w Łódż.

Thomas, A. (1985). *Grażyna Bacewicz Chamber and Orchestral Works*, Los Angeles: Friends of Polish Music, University of California.

Thomas, A. (2008). *Polish Music since Szymanowski*, Cambridge: Cambridge University Press.

Tokuda, T. (2016). 'Grażyna Bacewicz and Social Realism: A Stylistic Comparison of Piano Sonatas Nos. 1 and 2', DMA dissertation, University of Miami.

Watson, P. (1992). 'Gender Relations, Education and Social Change in Poland', *Gender and Education*, 4 (1–2), 127–47: www.academia.edu/2433940/ Gender_Relations_Education_and_Social_Change_in_Poland.

Zaimont, J. ed. (1994). *The Musical Woman: An International Perspective*, Westport, CT: Greenwood Press.

Primary Online Resources

Dla ludzi zawsze mam twarz pogodną . . . Grażyna Bacewicz (documentary film in Polish), directed by D. Pawelec, scenario by M. Gąsiorowska and D. Pawelec, Telewizja Polska – Program II 1999: www.youtube.com /watch?v=0HAGaACyt94.

Grażyna Bacewicz website at the Polish Music Information Centre, *Polmic.pl*: https://bacewicz.polmic.pl.

Lazar-Chmielowska, J. (2004). 'Grażyna Bacewicz – An Enduring Symbol of Polish Music', *Edukator.org.pl*: www.edukator.org.pl/2004b/symbol/symbol .html.

Polish Culture website, *Culture.pl*: https://culture.pl/en.

Polish Music Center website at The University of Southern California: https:// polishmusic.usc.edu/research/composers.

Sailow, S. & Kosanovic, V. (1976). 'Composer Grażyna Bacewicz', KPFA (Berkeley, CA), radio broadcast, 28 August 1976: http://servlet1 .lib.berkeley.edu:8080/audio/stream.play.logic?coll=pacifica&group= b23305539.

Thomas, A., *On Polish Music ... and Other Polish Topics*: https://onpolishmu sic.com/tag/adrian-thomas.University of Leipzig website, *The Letters of Grażyna Bacewicz to Vytautas Bacevičius (1945–1969: part 1)*, ed. Malgorzata Janicka-Slysz, translated by Jan Rybicki: www.gko.uni-leipzig.de/fileadmin/Fakultät_GKO/Musikwissenschaft/2.2-Forschung/ Musikerbriefe/18_1_JanSly1.pdf.

Acknowledgements

For their generous help, my grateful thanks go to the following individuals and
organizations for their generous help:

Rhiannon Mathias, Editor, CUP

Donna Cusack-Muller, Archivist, Australian Ballet Company

Jolanta Bonder, Archivist, Fryderyk Chopin University of Music, Warsaw

Butler School of Music, University of Texas

Prof. Pawel Lukaszewski, Vice Rector, Frederyk Chopin University of Music,
Warsaw

Colin Homiski, Research Librarian, Senate House Library, University of
London, WC1E 7HU

Magdalene Kaczmarek and Maciej Kabza, Librarians, Akademia Muzyczna
Grażyna i Kiejstuta Bacewiczów w Łódź, Poland

Photos from Polish Press Agency: www.pap.pl/en

Polish Music Information Centre: www.polmic.pl/index.php?lang=en

Jeremy Polmear, editorial suggestions

Polskie Wydawnictwo Muzyczne (PWM Edition)

Polish translation: Stefan Kasprzyk & Joanna Piotrowska

Photo usage permissions: Anastasia Lvov and Andrzej Szpilman

Reading the manuscript: Martha Kapos and Joanna Piotrowska

Warsaw photo from Anastasia Lvova

Henryk Wieniawski Violin Competition: www.wieniawski.com

Notes on Place Names

I have opted for the version of the place name with which the reader may be
more familiar. So, I've put in Warsaw rather than Warszawa, and think that
Kraków is recognisable, as is Łódź.

End Papers

Map of Poland 1939:

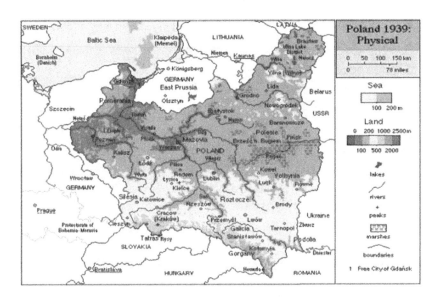

www.bing.com/images/search?view=detailV2&ccid=zfBMVtHF&id=
2C53E7F081A7ABA937843995E77F28D1CF29E50D&thid=OIP.zfBMV
tHFwx0PfIdIs57HkAAAAA&mediaurl=https%3a%2f%2fupload.wikimedia.org
%2fwikipedia%2fcommons%2fthumb%2f3%2f3b%2fPoland1939_physical.jpg
%2f400px-Poland1939_physical.jpg&exph=301&expw=400&q=map+of+poland
+in+1939&simid=608050352784739549&ck=3AA91FF32995169D229FE51
C02F92169&selectedIndex=2&FORM=IRPRST&ajaxhist=0

Map of Poland 1945:

www.bing.com/images/search?view=detailV2&ccid=xwP9e2Iz&id=98DC27
078BE13ACF51831DCA1F8EF97988455292&thid=OIP.xwP9e2IzJUPe
ONaVs18mewHaE3&mediaurl=https%3a%2f%2fwww.ushmm.org%2flcmedia%
2fmap%2flc%2fimage%2fpol71030.gif&exph=420&expw=640&q=
map+of+poland+in+1945&simid=608050593284688898&ck=BCACEFDF27
F78F3535D05C0BB2D07539&selectedIndex=6&FORM=IRPRST&ajaxhist=0

Cambridge Elements ⹀

Elements in Women in Music

Rhiannon Mathias
Bangor University

Dr. Rhiannon Mathias is Lecturer and Music Fellow in the School of Music and Media at Bangor University. She is the author of a number of women in music publications, including *Lutyens, Maconchy, Williams and Twentieth-Century British Music: A Blest Trio of Sirens* (2012), and gives frequent conference presentations, public lectures and radio broadcasts on the topic. She is also the editor of the Routledge Handbook on Women's Work in Music (forthcoming), a publication which arose from the First International Conference on Women's Work in Music (Bangor University, 2017), which she instigated and directed. The success of the first conference led to her directing a second conference in 2019.

About the Series

Elements in Women in Music provides an exciting and timely resource for an area of music scholarship which is undergoing rapid growth. The subject of music, women and culture is widely researched in the academy, and has also recently become the focus of much public debate in mainstream media.

This international series will bring together many different strands of research on women in classical and popular music. Envisaged as a multimedia digital 'stage' for showcasing new perspectives and writing of the highest quality, the series will make full use of online materials such as music sound links, audio and/or film materials (e.g. performances, interviews – with permission), podcasts and discussion forums relevant to chosen themes.

The series will appeal primarily to music students and scholars, but will also be of interest to music practitioners, industry professionals, educators and the general public.

Cambridge Elements☰

Elements in Women in Music

Elements in the Series

Grażyna Bacewicz, The First Lady of Polish Music
Diana Ambache

A full series listing is available at: www.cambridge.org/ewim

Printed in the United States
by Baker & Taylor Publisher Services